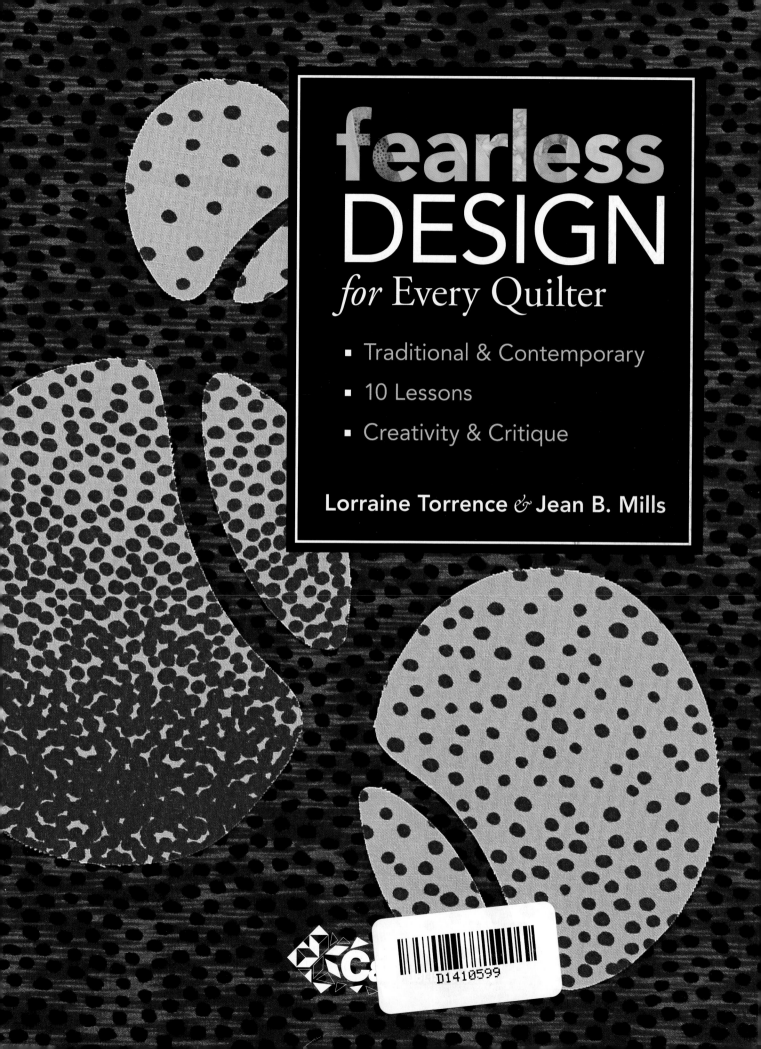

fearless DESIGN

for Every Quilter

- Traditional & Contemporary
- 10 Lessons
- Creativity & Critique

Lorraine Torrence *&* **Jean B. Mills**

Text and Artwork copyright © 2009 by Lorraine Torrence and Jean B. Mills

Artwork copyright © 2009 by C&T Publishing, Inc.

Publisher: Amy Marson

Creative Director: Gailen Runge

Editors: Lynn Koolish and Kesel Wilson

Technical Editors: Nanette S. Zeller and Ellen Pahl

Copyeditor/Proofreader: Wordfirm Inc.

Cover/Book Designer: Kristy K. Zacharias

Page Layout Artist: Kerry Graham

Production Coordinator: Zinnia Heinzmann

Illustrator: Richard Sheppard

Photography by Christina Carty-Francis and Diane Pedersen of C&T Publishing unless otherwise noted

Published by C&T Publishing, Inc., P.O. Box 1456, Lafayette, CA 94549

Library of Congress Cataloging-in-Publication Data

Torrence, Lorraine,

  Fearless design for every quilter : traditional & contemporary--10 lessons--creativity & critique / Lorraine Torrence and Jean B. Mills.

    p. cm.

  Includes bibliographical references.

  Summary: "The potential for creativity resides in everyone, but it needs development, through exercise and practice. The creativity exercises provided in this book are designed to help you tone your creative muscles. Each chapter is divided into three parts: the assignment, exercises, and the critique session"—Provided by publisher.

  ISBN 978-1-57120-576-6 (paper trade)

  1. Quilting. 2. Patchwork. 3. Quilts--Design. I. Mills, Jean B., II. Title.

  TT835.T663 2009

  746.46'041--dc22

                              2008030594

Printed in China

10 9 8 7 6 5 4 3 2 1

Dedication
From Lorraine
To Sharon Yenter, who was willing to give me the chance to try this kind of class in her quilt shop, and to the eager students who keep lining up to take it.

From Jean
To all my students and fiber art friends, who have provided a window into their creative processes, through which I could respectfully peer.

Acknowledgments

Lorraine and Jean wish to thank the following individuals:

The eight remarkable women who have been in Lorraine's long-term design class for over eight years and who so generously agreed to be the students in this book (You all were amazing—and on a tight schedule!)

Jane Koura, for providing photographs of all of the students

Craig Rowley, for generously allowing us to use two of his beautiful photographs for the Using Images from Your Surroundings chapter

The Art Institute of Chicago, the National Gallery of London, and the Fitzwilliam Museum at Cambridge University, for the use of the painting images for the master paintings exercise

Lynn Koolish and the rest of the C&T staff, for their trust that this would be a book worth publishing, and for all their help in making it happen

Lorraine wishes to thank her loving, flexible, and tolerant husband, Mike, for his help and patience during the writing of this book, and, in fact, all of the time; and all the thousands of quilting students since her first class in 1972, for helping her become a better teacher.

Jean wishes to thank Carl for his tireless support and love for 35 years, and Jacob and Rachel, who have always believed that she could do anything. She also wishes to thank her family and friends, especially Anne, Barry, Pam, and Peggy, who have given their special support for this project.

contents

laying *the* groundwork

Read this section first to understand how to best use this book. You'll learn about the creative process and the critique process, and meet the students who bring the lessons in this book to life.

Introduction

In 1971, Jonathan Holstein and Gail van der Hoof organized an exhibition of American pieced quilts at the Whitney Museum of American Art in New York City. This exhibition, which reignited interest in quiltmaking, focused strictly on the quilts' artistic merits and visual impact, and, for the first time, displayed quilts on the walls of a museum, as paintings are displayed.

Since then, quiltmakers, both traditional and innovative, have awakened to the realization that quilting is an art form and requires some sense of color and design to be successful. A few quilters have formal training in art, many have intuitive art sensibilities, and more are increasingly seeking classes to help them learn and develop an understanding of design in order to improve their quilts.

This book is based on one such class: a long-term design class for quilters that Lorraine Torrence has been teaching since 1997.

The Design Essentials Class

Lorraine

In 1997, Lorraine began teaching an ongoing design class for quilters. Her perception was that quilters were feeling the need for more in-depth education in design and wanted more than the usual short, simplified class. Few, however, were ready to go back to college for a four-year degree in art or design. The result was a nine-month-long class that met once a month for three hours. The focus was to teach design using exercises and to provide instruction in effective critique. Assignments on the elements and principles of design were sketches only, not finished work. This eliminated pressure and inhibition while encouraging experimentation. Assignments were given with minimal instruction and explanation. The students were asked to think about what the assignment really meant and how they might interpret it. With the help of a suggested reading list and a handout on basic design terms, the students went home to interpret the assignment. Some worked all month on the assignment, while others started the night before the next class.

When twenty students came back to the next class, twenty completely different solutions to the assignment were presented. A critique session examined each student's interpretation of the assignment and clarified the design principles and elements central to the exercise. The students learned to talk about what they saw, evaluate how successfully the principles were applied, and offer and receive constructive critiques. Trust was built, skills grew, and work improved. The class was a success and the students wanted more.

Lorraine developed a second-level class with exercises focusing more on design sources and inspiration. The principles from the first course were constantly reinforced in the new exercises.

Now there are three levels to Lorraine's classes: Design I (Principles and Elements), Design II (Sources and Inspiration), and Design III (Independent or Guided Series Work). Many students enroll in these courses and produce sophisticated work. They increase their skill and become more comfortable with critique. Quilters are hungry to learn more about design, to work hard, and to improve their skills. This book is a summation of the three courses, focusing on exercises in design, critique, and the creative process.

Jean

Jean met Lorraine when she signed up as a student in Lorraine's Design Essentials class. Jean took the class to increase her own satisfaction with her fiber artwork. Already a quilter, Jean knew that learning about design in a class where she could share, take design risks, and receive helpful critique from a community was the kind of learning environment she needed. As her knowledge of design increased, an unexpected additional learning occurred.

As an art therapist, Jean became fascinated observing the growth in the students as seen through their work and the information about the processes they shared. As their confidence grew, so did their exploration of new creative approaches. Of particular interest was the fact that while seeking solutions to the same design problem given in class, individuals returned with unique outcomes that never resembled any other student's work. Exposure to others' ideas created a kind of synergy from which original ideas seemed to spring freely. The students not only valued their own work, but also placed special importance on creativity and its role in their lives. Jean's portion of this book collaboration is a result of these observations and conversations with the students, combined with her understanding and knowledge of psychology and the human creative spirit.

You are holding the result of Lorraine and Jean's collaboration. As you look through the pages, read the words of the eight women students who share their journeys and wisdom. Throughout the book, you will be encouraged to explore the design exercises, take risks, and develop your own critique group or design community.

Our Goals in Writing This Book

Our goals in writing this book are to cover three major categories: design, critique, and creativity. Growth in these three categories accelerates when the three are developed in concert.

Design

In all visual art, there are design fundamentals that anyone can learn. However, learning requires practice. The more you practice these fundamentals, the more skilled you will become.

Good design is the result of a successful combination of **design elements** (color, value, line, shape, pattern, and texture) and **design principles** (balance, unity, emphasis, composition, variety, and scale). It is the concepts of these elements and principles that we present for your study.

Use the exercises in this book to design your quilts and textile art more skillfully. Be patient. The successful use of design principles and elements is not something you can learn in one afternoon. We encourage you to learn, practice, learn more, and practice even more.

Critique

Language helps you clarify and define what is in your head. If you learn to articulate your vague and intuitive senses, you will build on these intuitions and solidify the concepts in your thought processes. Verbal interaction broadens your exposure and your experience. Developing the language of design is the first step in participating in critique.

Critique differs from criticism in that it is objective and helpful. Criticism is subjective, disapproving, and usually hurtful. Listening to the comments of our students in this book—eavesdropping on their critique sessions as they study each other's exercises—will, we hope, encourage you to form your own assessments and virtually join the critique group. Perhaps you and your friends will be stimulated to start your own critique group. Trust, enlightenment, and confidence are sure to ensue. Even on your own, you can use the lessons and techniques in this book to critique your own work and expand your design horizons. We hope our students will encourage you as they share revelations about their own creative journeys and processes.

Creativity

You may think that creative genius is something a person is born with. Nothing could be further from the truth. The **potential** for creativity resides in everyone, but it needs development, through exercise and practice. Olympic athletes spend many hours every day keeping their muscles toned and strong by doing repetitive exercises that may not even seem related to their sport. Keeping your creativity in optimum condition

come join in the learning!

> "Imagination grows by exercise, and contrary to common belief, is more powerful in the mature than in the young."
> – W. Somerset Maugham

takes work and practice, too. The creativity exercises we've provided in this book are designed to help you tone your creative muscles.

How to Use This Book

Read the chapters on the creative process (pages 8–10) and the critique process (pages 11–12). Then move through the rest of the book, beginning with the first five exercises in Design Principles and Elements (starting on page 16). Follow this with the next set of five exercises in the Design Sources and Inspiration section (starting on page 52). Then finally, continue your learning by following the process for working in a series (starting on page 80).

Each of the exercise chapters is divided into three parts:

- The assignment is presented in a way that does not fully explain or give you all the information about the subject in advance—we've found that people learn more when they work to figure out the solution themselves, perhaps even doing a little research. This approach also increases the variety of interpretations among the students in the class. This variety broadens the

students' exposure and experience when we compare the finished exercises in the critique session.

We suggest that you interpret the work as exercises rather than finished work. Creating finished work often comes with pressure that results in stifled experimentation. The goal in doing the exercises is not to create a masterpiece but rather to learn something. Remember, the more **you** practice, the more you learn! Take time to think how you might interpret the exercise before you look at the students' solutions.

Construction Options

Exercises may be fused or basted to a foundation, ironed to a fusible interfacing (which eliminates the need for fusible web and foundation), glued to paper, pieced, or appliquéd. We prefer the quick fusible methods, so that the focus remains on the design process, not the assembly technique. However, feel free to use the method of your choice.

- The critique session follows each assignment, with photos of finished exercises from three or four of our students. In a live critique session, the maker of the piece presents her thoughts and experiences first. In our chapters, this is usually only a brief description of what she presented and some personal feedback about the process. Following this initial introduction of the work, other students and the teacher offer their observations and critiques. You will find differences of opinion throughout the critique sessions. Discussing diverse points of view during a critique session is a form of brainstorming and helps in future decision making and fine-tuning of the design process. Indeed, there may be a variety of good solutions to every problem. Exposure to approaches unlike your own will broaden your perceptions.

- The continuing education process, which follows the critique session, summarizes and clarifies some of the lessons in the assignment. Within the continuing education process, Lorraine provides an **additional design exercise** and Jean adds a **creativity exercise** to keep your ideas flowing. A **suggested reading** list concludes each exercise. Some of the books listed are unfortunately out of print, but reference copies can sometimes be found in public or guild libraries, or used copies might be purchased on the Internet or from used book stores.

COMMIT TO CREATE:
The Creative Process

Many people believe that creativity is a magical power limited to those who have a special talent. Scientific evidence shows us that this is a myth. Being creative is not a mysterious process understood by only a few. Rather, it is a process in which anyone can engage and produce new ideas. The secret is work, trial and error, and learning from mistakes.

People engage in the creative process for many reasons and with widely varying results. Children create because they believe they can. They are imaginative, playful, curious, and willing to take risks. Adults do not lose the ability to create; they merely lose the ability to believe.

66 Every child is an artist. The problem is how to remain an artist, once we grow up." – Pablo Picasso

Many times, we have heard people say, "Oh, I'm not creative" or "When I try to create something, it never turns out right." Merely trying to encourage these people and reassure them frequently just reinforces the "no, I can't" belief. Their frustration comes not because they truly aren't creative but because they just don't know how to access and develop the creativity that lies dormant in them.

66 Any reaction to stimulus may be causally explained, but the creative act, which is the absolute antithesis to mere reaction, will forever elude the human understanding." – Carl G. Jung

The amazing thing about the creative process is that about 90% of it can be learned, but one has to **commit** to do the work. A new creative solution can't illuminate the light-bulb unless you have carefully laid the wires through which the new idea can flow. Thomas Edison once said, "Genius is 1% inspiration and 99% perspiration."

Getting Started

The following steps will begin to explain how the creative process works and what you can do to actively engage in it successfully. Get ready! In following these steps, you'll have to take risks, be playful, and be ready to experience the countless rewards of opening up your creative self.

> **the steps to creativity**
>
> ### 1. PREPARE
> Gather information, ideas, and inspiration.
>
> ### 2. INCUBATE
> Digest all you have gathered.
>
> ### 3. CREATE
> Put your ideas in motion with new solutions to design challenges.
>
> ### 4. EVALUATE
> Assess your work and document your assessment.

Adapted from Graham Wallace, 1926

 Creativity, as has been said, consists of largely rearranging what we know in order to find out what we do not know." – George Kneller

1. PREPARE

This is where the work begins. Success depends on your **commitment** to learning by **doing**.

- Create a space in which you can work. Surround yourself with things that inspire and stimulate your creativity: fabric, yarn, beads, colored pencils, drawing tools, paper, books, pictures, your camera, and so on.

- Expand your experiences and draw from them to help generate new ideas. Immerse yourself in experiences that will stimulate and inspire you. Engage in the creative process. Learn all the new techniques you can. Read, take classes, go to galleries, expose yourself to the work of others, travel, take photos, and join groups of people who share similar artistic interests.

- Stock up on ideas. Keep an inspiration journal where you collect and catalog ideas and images that inspire you. Make notes to yourself about color, texture, and feelings associated with your inspirations.

- Generate new ideas. Carry your camera and your sketchbook with you everywhere you go. Use your own work as a starting point.

- Practice the process. Spend time every day creating.

- Clear time to create. Time constraints kill creative flow.

- Practice affirmations on a daily basis. Remind yourself that there is a fearless, creative child in you who wants to play and create.

2. INCUBATE

- Incubation is the time when **you just let go** and allow the information, inspiration, and daily practice to come together in the subconscious. You have been doing the work and now it is about to pay off! If you are feeling a block, be patient and trust. Trying to force creative ideas is like trying to push a river—it expends a lot of energy but it doesn't work. Creative juices are always flowing; be aware of ideas as they hatch.

 Action will remove the doubt that theory cannot solve."
– Tehyi Hsieh, *Chinese Epigrams Inside and Out*

3. CREATE

- The challenge! It's now time to bring your ideas together with your ability to create.

The original idea starts taking shape as a piece of tangible fiber art.

There are two kinds of creators, the visualizer and the intuitor:

> *The visualizer* is a person who sees the outcome before she or he begins the process. The finished piece is not a surprise; it is the manifestation of the idea and careful planning. If you are a planner, don't be afraid to let the materials have their way once in a while.
>
> *The intuitor* allows the process and materials to take her or him to an end product. This person is usually surprised by the outcome. My research tells me that for this kind of creative person, planning actually gets in the way of her process or squelches it entirely. If you are an intuitive creator, don't be afraid to start with a general plan once in a while.

Regardless which type of creator you are, remember that trying new approaches to your process can lead you to new discoveries.

Both of these ways are the right way; they are both equally valid. Though they appear quite different in process, the outcomes are equally original, possess integrity, and have artistic merit.

- Avoid self-criticism because it will cut off the flow of creative energy. Play is a good way to quiet the critical self. If you get in a creative logjam, don't be afraid to put a piece down for a time and go to work on another.

- Make decisions and put them in motion. Laboring over each decision is another way to stay stuck in one place. Acknowledge whatever is keeping you from taking a risk or making a decision and moving forward. Ask yourself, "What is the worst thing that can happen if I make a mistake?" When you make a mistake, learn from it.

- Experiment as you go. New discoveries are the happy outcome of experimentation.

- Every person's style is different. Your own creative voice, or style, is what makes your ideas and work recognizable and unique. Don't worry if you don't seem to have a particular voice yet; some voices just take longer to develop.

The sense of being lost in time is called flow and is the optimal creative experience. You forget your bodily self and leave the critic behind. Flow is like a river of creative energy coming from a place deep within. It feels wonderful!

4. EVALUATE

After you have finished your piece, it is important to the process that you take time to evaluate the outcome. Evaluation should not be confused with criticism. In evaluating your work, you affirm that there is value in what you have created.

- Personal evaluation involves asking yourself questions such as the following:

Do you like it?

Based on what you have learned about design, have you used your skills well?

What is strong, and what would make the design stronger?

What would you avoid doing again?

Did you make any new discoveries?

Is this piece one that would lend itself to a series? If so, where would you go next?

Be sure to document your evaluation.

- Critique groups are good communities in which to share your work. They are designed to support you and your process. One of their important tasks is to give honest, useful feedback to the artist. They also provide an opportunity for you to learn more about your work by seeing and giving feedback on other artists' work. It's a win-win for everyone. This kind of group is not show-and-tell; it demands a willingness to give and receive fearless, constructive, and thoughtful feedback (not criticism) about the pieces presented.

Creativity is about not only ability and bringing new ideas to fruition, but also having a social group see your work to affirm your process. Sometimes this is done by entering it into an exhibition or show.

Creative ability is not reserved for a gifted few. If you are in doubt about your abilities, follow the steps through the creative process. This journey can give you a way to see your capabilities and provide opportunities to focus on your work. So, get started! If you already create regularly, this chapter should reinforce and remind you what you need to do to keep going. You will learn more about yourself as an artist and make your life richer by actively engaging in a process that will provide creative energy and pleasure in return.

Suggested Reading

Bayles, David, and Ted Orland. *Art and Fear: Observations on the Perils (and Rewards) of Artmaking*. Saint Paul, MN: Image Continuum Press, 1993.

Cameron, Julia. *The Artist's Way: Spiritual Path to Higher Creativity*. 10th ed. New York: Penguin Putnam, 1992.

Edwards, Betty. *Drawing on the Artist Within*. New York: Simon & Schuster, 1986.

Getlein, Mark. *Living with Art*. 7th ed. New York: McGraw-Hill, 2005.

Kneller, George F. *The Art and Science of Creativity*. New York: Holt, Rinehart and Winston, 1965.

London, Peter. *No More Secondhand Art: Awakening the Artist Within*. Boston: Shambhala Publications, 1989.

McNiff, Shaun. *Art Heals: How Creativity Cures the Soul*. Boston: Shambhala Publications, 2004.

Shahn, Ben. *The Shape of Content*. New York: Vintage Books, 1960.

The Critique Process

An important component when studying design is to learn to understand, analyze, and evaluate what you see when you look at your own and others' work. Doing this in a supportive class or critique group is immensely helpful. Sharing questions, comments, and opinions about exercises or finished work functions like brainstorming. It exposes points of view you may not have considered and can help you notice even more about the work. Even without a group, critiquing your own work will help you develop a critical eye and expand your design skills.

Vocabulary

Learning to talk about design elements and principles is essential if you are critiquing art. Simply adding new words to your vocabulary can open up new understanding. The vocabulary of design includes words you may know and some that may be unfamiliar. The following design components and related terminology are used in the exercises in this book:

- Color: What we see when light is reflected off an object; also known as hue

- Value: The relative lightness or darkness of a color

- Scale: The relative size and arrangement of various objects, or printed fabric motifs, in comparison to other objects or printed motifs in the same work

- Unity: The sense of harmony that comes when all the parts of a work look like they belong together

- Balance: The sense of equality and stability in the visual weight of objects in a piece of work, so that the viewer's attention is directed around the work in a pattern rather than being skewed in a particular direction or jumping around randomly

Vocabulary is not limited to the words that define the elements and principles of design. Useful vocabulary extends to **how** we talk about work in a critique session.

Phrasing Critique Comments

Compare the following two comments:

1. "I don't like the way you put so much solid dark brown at the bottom left side of the quilt."

2. "If the dark brown were repeated in the upper right-hand corner of the quilt, perhaps it would help the balance. Replacing the solid brown with a mottled brown or a brown print might also provide some visual texture that would create movement and interest."

In the first comment, the viewer simply expresses dislike and criticism. Liking or not liking the piece is not the point of the critique. Saying **why** you like or dislike the piece is what is useful. In the second comment, the viewer suggests some alternatives that might improve the imbalance and the flatness of the solid brown in the quilt.

The maker of the quilt might even evaluate her own work in two different ways:

1. "This was my first attempt at this exercise. I really hated it. The second one works."

2. "In my first attempt, there were too many disparate techniques used together. In the second attempt, I used similar techniques so the styles of each part of the quilt worked together."

The second comment clarifies for the maker, and for the rest of the critique group, why the first quilt design didn't work and what made the second quilt design more successful.

We can all look at a quilt and say, "Wow! I really like your quilt!" but no one has learned anything from that comment. In a really productive critique session, the goal is trying to define what works, what doesn't, and why.

The Discussion Leader

After the formation of a critique group, it is useful for someone to take on the role of discussion leader. In a class, this is usually the teacher. The maker of each piece should be given the opportunity to speak first. There are usually some oohs and ahs when the work is first shown, but the maker can lay the groundwork by telling how she approached the exercise or what ideas generated the piece, what techniques she used, and what problems or surprises she encountered as she worked through her piece. It is always interesting to hear about the message or content of the work too, but this information usually does not—or should not—engender critical comments other than in relation to how effectively the formal qualities contribute to the task of conveying the intent of the designer. The leader can then invite the group to comment using the useful questions listed below. The leader should also control negative comments and keep track of time to keep the critique session on track.

Useful Questions

When the critique session is slow getting started, the discussion leader can ask questions to help. The following questions could be helpful:

- How is the use of value in this piece? Is there enough contrast to see the design? Is this high contrast or low contrast?

- Do you think this piece is balanced? What kind of balance did the maker employ in designing this piece?

- Is this piece visually unified? What devices did the maker use to create visual unity?

The Critical Eye

Jill Pollard, in her article "The Critical Eye" (*American Quilter* XI, Spring 1995, pages 26–31), defines the critique process as four key steps. The discussion leader can help direct the discussion using those key steps.

1. Describe: Use the language of design to describe the formal elements you see.

2. Analyze: Focus on the design principles, and analyze the composition. Do the formal elements contribute to the success of the design?

3. Interpret: Listen to the artist talk about her intent or meaning. Do the visual elements support the content?

4. Respond: It is inevitable and appropriate to talk about how you feel about the quilt, but try to identify what makes you feel that way.

To Ask or Not to Ask

Sometimes an artist will bring a work in process just to show the group what she's doing. She is feeling good enough about it to consider entering it in a judged and juried show. In this case, she should ask the group not to make any comments in the form of suggestions to improve or change the work. Pieces entered in judged and juried shows should be independent, uninfluenced work. Class work done under the tutelage, guidance, or influence of a teacher or other students' opinions is inappropriate as an entry in a judged and juried show. Reserve critique for those who **want** critique.

If you do ask for critique, be prepared to hear different opinions. You will read some critique comments in the exercise chapters that vary widely. The comments are bound to reflect the different experiences, observation skills, and preferences of the viewers. Consider all comments with respect, and use what makes sense to you and has some resonance for you. Learn from everything. Paying attention to what others see sharpens your own vision.

Meet the Students

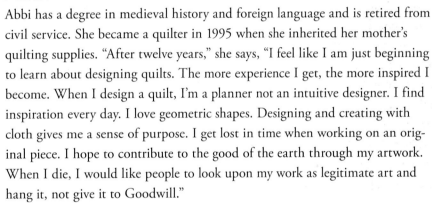

The following eight students are representative of the people who take Lorraine's design classes. Their work and thoughts appear as examples of design and critique. As you'll read, they have varied backgrounds and approaches to creating. Some are full-time artists; some work full-time at other jobs and squeeze in creative time whenever they can. All of them are committed to the creative process and share their learning experiences in this book.

Abbi

Abbi has a degree in medieval history and foreign language and is retired from civil service. She became a quilter in 1995 when she inherited her mother's quilting supplies. "After twelve years," she says, "I feel like I am just beginning to learn about designing quilts. The more experience I get, the more inspired I become. When I design a quilt, I'm a planner not an intuitive designer. I find inspiration every day. I love geometric shapes. Designing and creating with cloth gives me a sense of purpose. I get lost in time when working on an original piece. I hope to contribute to the good of the earth through my artwork. When I die, I would like people to look upon my work as legitimate art and hang it, not give it to Goodwill."

Abbi Barden
Photo by Cassie Barden

Amalia

"I designed and dyed the fabric for my first art quilt in 1991," Amalia says. This was the start of what has become a meaningful and passionate journey. From 1992 to 1994 she served in the Peace Corps in West Africa and collected African textiles. "I enjoy working with richly textured fabrics in quilts," she explains. "I started in Lorraine's design course in 1998. The design concepts I learned and applied to my work allowed me to start thinking of myself as a designer. In 2001, I completed my PhD in biostatistics. My day job is very logic-oriented and its product is intangible. On the weekends in my studio, I play with fabric and create art quilts as a counterbalance to my job. Creating art is confidence building for me. That confidence is part of me when I leave my studio, and it goes with me into my daily life."

Amalia Magaret
Photo by Steven I. Gorwitz

Bonny

Bonny is a genetics professor in genome sciences at the University of Washington. She has loved art since childhood. She only wishes she had discovered art quilting earlier. She plans many of her quilts in her head or on the computer before she begins. "I get my best ideas when showering or when sleeping," she says. "I love figuring out how to put a piece together—how to solve problems—so it would spoil the fun to read about how someone else solved similar problems."

Some of her inspiration comes from microscopic images of cells she sees in her scientific life. Her artistic goal is to create a piece that shows the viewer something he or she may never have seen before, or to show it in a new way, perhaps with a bit of surprise.

Bonny Brewer
Photo by Barbara Fox

Cindy

Cindy's family moved more than 25 times when she was growing up. "We would sell everything, and each person got one suitcase," she recalls. "My mother always insisted that the sewing machine come along. My grandmother had worked for one of the big Hollywood studios. She told of the feather dresses she would make for Ginger Rogers, and how they had to use the thread from the fabric itself to sew the clothes. After escaping (graduating) high school, I taught myself how to play several musical instruments. After a stressful day, playing the piano was like 'letting the cork out.' It's like that for me now with quilting. My work is original and I work intuitively. I get inspiration from my design classes. The critique sessions are the most important for me. Feedback helps me better evaluate my work. I feel that without the critique it's just a show-and-tell, and I can't learn from that."

Cindy Hayes
Photo by David K. Beckman

Jane

Jane is a retired government employee whose passion in life is creating with fiber. "Creating is not a choice for me," she states. "It's a necessity." She is a longtime student of design and has studied with many prominent teachers in the field of fiber art who have stimulated, encouraged, and inspired her. Jane's approach to her work is intuitive and fearless. She has created a studio space that is full of inspiration, including her neon Open sign. "My studio gives me a feeling of credibility," she explains. Jane says the act of creating helps her gain control over our complex world. "My goal in life is not to hang my work in galleries," she says, "but to show my daughters that it is important to have a 'room of one's own.'"

Jane Koura
Photo by Jane Koura

Marj

Marj is the owner of a salon and is a semi-retired hairdresser. She also is caregiver for two of her family members. Despite the demands on her time and emotions, Marj strongly states that no matter what life dishes out, she believes happiness is a choice. "I get great happiness from going into my studio daily and working on my fiber art," she says. "It's play for me. I center my life by balancing my energy coming in and going out. I didn't learn to do this until I was an adult. I have learned that opportunities can come from difficulties. I believe this is a universal principle. My art helps me survive; seldom do I let anything pull me away from it. I feel alive when I am working in my studio. I never want to stop learning and creating."

Marj Brost
Photo by Jane Koura

Ruth

Ruth enjoys studying how environment, including art, affects humans. Her work as an artist is influenced by culture. She holds a master's degree in anthropology and museum studies and has been a museum curator. She has also achieved a certificate in art and design from the City and Guilds program developed in England. She has traveled to Japan and the Middle East and remarks, "Travel provides me with inspiration through understanding a culture and its art. I sketch when I travel and later may use those sketches as design inspiration for my own fiber art compositions."

Ruth Vincent
Photo by Craig Rowley

Sharon

Sharon has a BS in physics and an MBA, and recently completed a fiber arts certificate program. She began quilting in 1990 and has always designed original pieces. After 25 years in the world of finance, she is now completely involved in her work as a fiber artist. "My work has to have something that is more than just images," she says. "It has to have a spiritual connection to me. I feel I can give a message of hope through my quilts. My goal for my art is to have it seen. I am not interested in selling it or making it pretty; I just want it to be respectful of the message I hope to express."

Sharon Rowley
Photo by Craig Rowley

design principles *and* elements

The first part of the design course focuses on design principles and elements, exploring the relationship of these components to the overall success of a quilt design.

Balance

The principle of balance is an important consideration in designing a quilt. The four main types of balance used are **symmetrical, radial, crystallographic,** and **asymmetrical.** The following exercise will introduce you to these principles and allow you to explore how they relate to the design process.

Symmetrical Balance

Symmetrical balance, or symmetry, is the regular arrangement of similar parts in a predictable pattern. Ruth McDowell, in her book *Symmetry*, explains that there are seventeen different kinds of symmetry based on the scientific study of crystallography. For purposes of our exercises in balance, we will limit our symmetry choices to five. By its very nature, symmetry is balanced.

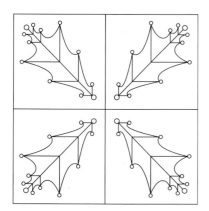

Rotational symmetry Each quarter of the design is the same but is rotated 90°.

Mirror symmetry on a vertical axis The left is the mirror image of the right.

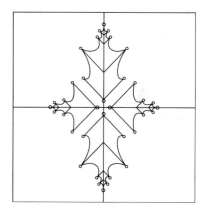

Mirror symmetry on vertical and horizontal axes The top mirrors the bottom and the left mirrors the right.

Translational symmetry Unsymmetrical motifs are arranged in identical rows.

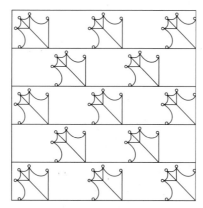

Shifted rows symmetry For each row, the design is repeated but shifted horizontally.

Radial Balance

Radial balance is based on elements radiating from a central point. In quilting, some traditional blocks are based on grid divisions (like four-patch and nine-patch blocks) and others are based on divisions of a circle (Dresden Plate and Winding Ways). Radial balance is based on divisions of a circle. To achieve radial balance, it's best to use five or more divisions. Using just four divisions would be the same as rotational symmetry (see above).

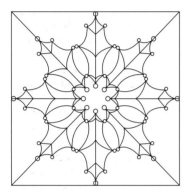

Radial balance The design is repeated around the center axis.

Crystallographic Balance

Crystallographic balance is a field of pattern scattered all over the surface. Essentially, it is balance without a focal point. It is balanced because it is the same all over.

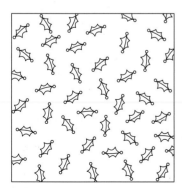

Crystallographic balance The design is balanced without a focal point.

Asymmetrical Balance

Asymmetrical balance is more difficult to explain. In asymmetrical balance, parts of a composition are not the same but are balanced in placement and visual weight. Think of a teeter-totter. Two people of equal weight in the same position on each end represent symmetrical balance. Two people of unequal weight with the heavier person moved closer to the fulcrum or balance point can also balance the teeter-totter; this is asymmetrical balance—equal but not the same.

Another way to achieve asymmetrical balance would be to place one heavy person on one side and two people, each half the weight of the heavy person, in the same spot on the other end of the teeter-totter. Of course, there are many variables to our heavy and light people analogy, both in placement and in number, that would achieve asymmetrical balance. The thing to keep in mind is that asymmetry can be balanced or not balanced, depending on how you arrange the parts of your composition in terms of size, number of elements, value, and color. Balance is achieved by equalizing the visual weight of elements that are not the same.

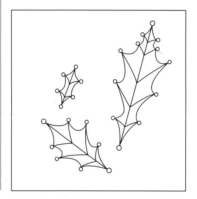

Asymmetrical balance The design is balanced by its arrangement of parts. The visual weight of the elements is equalized in the arrangement.

the assignment

Refer to the Introduction (page 7) for construction options.

1. Choose a theme shape or motif (a geometric shape, leaf, hand, house, or the like).

2. Interpret the shape or motif in at least 4 different compositions using different types of balance: 1 composition using one kind of symmetrical balance, and 3 compositions, each using one of the other 3 types of balance described above.

3. Make each composition about 20″ × 20″ square. Other than the theme shape or motif, you may want to give your compositions some additional unifying factor (color, fabric, technique, and so on.).

the critique session

ABBI struggled to decide on a shape she felt would work in the exercises. She finally chose the arrow after seeing one on a road sign. "Inspiration is all around us!" said Abbi. Since some of the symmetry concepts were new to her, she studied the assignment carefully. Once she understood the concepts, she found the individual exercises easy to design. "I loved doing this project!" she exclaimed.

Rotational symmetry All four quadrants of this piece are the same, and if rotated 90° would still be the same. Abbi's work certainly satisfied the balance assignment. Most of the group thought adding more color would give the piece additional excitement. Bonny, Jane, and Marj all commented on the interesting positive/negative effect achieved when the focus shifts from light blue arrows on a dark background to dark blue squares on a light blue background.

Radial balance Everyone agreed that this piece was radially balanced and interesting in color and value. There was disagreement about whether the large blue arrows should have been another color. Some thought their color too close in value to the background; a more contrasting color would have made them more noticeable. Others found the blue arrows interestingly subtle in creating a negative space. Comments about the red corner triangles were that they "brought the brighter colors out to the edge," keeping the whole surface important and creating an interesting "folded back" effect, and that their shape "mimicked the head of the arrows, drawing the eye outward."

> ❝❝ Abbi's pieces show how asymmetrical balance can give the impression of movement while symmetrical balance is often quite static." – Ruth

Translational symmetry Abbi intended this to be her interpretation of crystallographic balance, but the group thought it was actually translational symmetry. To make it crystallographic, Abbi could have made the arrows much smaller and scattered them randomly over the surface instead of placing them in tidy rows. But whatever balance principle it represented, everyone thought this was a successful piece with its rich, subtle color and interesting value changes.

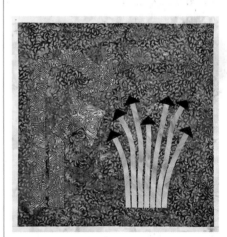

Asymmetrical balance There was consensus that this piece was asymmetrical, but not all thought it was balanced. Some thought the large green arrows were too close in value to the background to balance the piece; others felt the size of the subtle green arrows added enough visual weight to create the necessary balance. Cindy thought a different background color and print would have allowed the arrows to do their work better. But the whimsy of the piece did not go unnoticed by the group. Cindy said it evoked a "Blue Angels, ace fliers" look.

AMALIA is inspired by the colors in the leaves on her autumn morning runs, so choosing a motif was easy for her. She traced some actual leaves and prepared the shapes with fusible backing to iron onto strip-pieced backgrounds. She felt the crystallographic and asymmetrical pieces were the most successful because they seemed more natural and moved the eye over the surface better.

Mirror symmetry on a vertical axis The diagonal piecing in the background is more suited to the mirror symmetry in this piece than it was to the rotational symmetry at left. However, some felt the high-contrast background kept this piece from exhibiting true mirror symmetry. An actual mirror placed on the vertical centerline would reveal that the sides don't exactly match. Amalia compensated for the heavy dark value on the left by placing light leaves on that side and dark leaves on the light background on the right. Several members of the group thought this adequately balanced the piece.

Rotational symmetry The placement of Amalia's leaf shapes is certainly rotationally balanced, but about half the group felt that the stark contrast and the angles of the stripes in the background kept the piece from being balanced in a rotational way.

Crystallographic balance Everyone agreed that this piece showed successful crystallographic balance. Jane's comment was that even though some of the leaves were larger and darker than others, there were enough of them so that they didn't create a strong focal point. Everyone found this piece appealing, both in its composition and in how it captured the breezy feeling of falling leaves.

66 In all of Amalia's pieces, I enjoy the contrast of the changing values in the straight pieced backgrounds and the playful quality of the blowing and falling leaves." – Cindy

Asymmetrical balance The consensus was that in this piece the lighter pile of leaves on the bottom was balanced by the few dark leaves on the gradually lightening background strips at the upper left of the piece. Lorraine felt that if one or two of the lighter leaves at the bottom left were moved to the bottom right to make that side of the leaf pile a little higher, it might help balance the visually weighty upper left corner.

RUTH delighted everyone with her boats. The secondary pattern that emerged in the rotationally balanced sailboats surprised and pleased her, as did the propeller image that emerged in the radial balance piece. Ruth confessed that she would have liked to see something less static in her mirror symmetry of the ship.

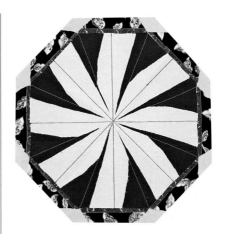

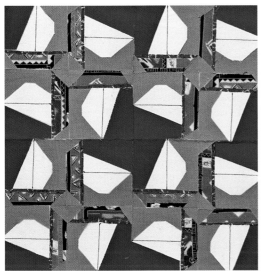

Rotational symmetry This is a good example of rotational symmetry: the piece can be repeatedly rotated 90°, and with each turn the composition stays the same. Cindy and Sharon both commented on the importance of the mast line as well as the brown hull in creating a pinwheel in each quadrant of the quilt. Cindy also noticed that the two different colors of blue created a secondary pattern that added to the complexity and interest of the piece.

Radial balance Ruth created an abstract pattern in her radial composition of sailboats. Cindy saw the red and brown lines of the hull of the boat as a border around the fan of sails in the center. This strong design appealed to most of the group.

> ❝ I love the motif of the boat and the way Ruth has morphed it into a ship in two of the pieces. Both warm and cool blues add richness to the palette."
> – Bonny

Mirror symmetry on a vertical axis The conversion of the motif to the ocean liner was a natural for the use of mirror symmetry. The word "powerful" arose more than once in the comments of the group in regard to this interpretation. The fact that Ruth used the entire height of the picture plane to show the ship's head-on symmetry, rather than showing sky space at the top and sea space at the bottom, added to the power and imposing nature of the piece. This ship is upon us, and we can't ignore it!

Asymmetrical balance This piece was the favorite of the group as a whole. The asymmetrical balance was achieved by the placement of the large light area at the top of the ship on the left and the sails of the two smaller boats on the right. Ruth added more light to the small boats in the white-caps of the waves to clinch the balance of the light placement. Bonny and Cindy noticed the effective use of the wake line of the ship to create a sense of depth, which was reinforced by the diminishing size of the sailboat in the background. The wake line also repeated the V-shape in the design of the ship, strengthening the unity.

JANE chose this more organic arrow so she would have the chance to create some curves. She photocopied the shape she drew, then enlarged and reduced it to create patterns for fusing the arrows onto a background. The group loved the rich color palette Jane used with her lively arrows, but there was disagreement about the effectiveness of the black-and-white checked fabric in two of the pieces. Some thought it added zing and contrast to the solids, but Bonny felt it didn't add to either composition.

Radial symmetry The subtle kaleidoscopic center as well as the octagonal shape of the piece helps define its radial symmetry, but Abbi would have liked to see more crispness in the definition of the shapes. Amalia thought more contrast in the values would make the piece more defined. Everyone found the liveliness of the shape exciting and engaging. However, Cindy commented that all the arrows pointed in and when her eye got to the center, she would have liked to see something more interesting there.

> 66 I think Jane's design is very effective because the intermittent dark spaces keep it from being too much the same." – Bonny

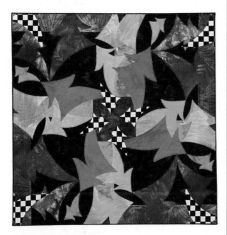

Rotational symmetry The black-and-white checked fabric in this piece helps identify the rotational balance—each black-and-white checked piece is clearly repeated four times in each of the corners and again in the center. Ruth liked the complexity of the layered effect, which made the four sections less obvious, while Sharon thought the busyness of the overlapping shapes and the checkerboard almost hid the symmetry. Everyone recognized the rotational symmetry, but personal taste, as it applied to other qualities in the piece, left the group without agreement on the success of the piece.

Crystallographic balance Although there is variety in the sizes and colors of the arrows, there is no actual grid or focal point, keeping the balance crystallographic. Even the blank rectangles do not stand out as focal points that are noticeably different from the rest. Of Jane's balance pieces, Amalia liked this one best—she thought the light, medium, and dark values, as well as the vibrant colors, were nicely distributed.

Asymmetrical balance The centers of the three arrow flowers in Jane's asymmetrical piece form focal points that keep the eye moving in a triangle around the piece. Cindy thought the composition of the background also supported the asymmetry of the piece. The change in the sizes of the arrow flowers adds to the asymmetry of the composition.

the continuing education process

The following question often arises about the difference between structure and visual appearance in balance: If a composition is made up of a regular, symmetrical pattern in its structure or pieced parts, but it is colored asymmetrically, is it symmetrical or asymmetrical?

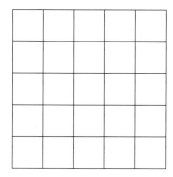

A design that is symmetrical in its seam structure

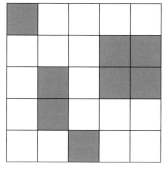

The same design colored asymmetrically

Would you agree about the symmetry and asymmetry in these examples?

For quilting art, with its built-in dual characteristics of the visual and the structural, the consensus is that the visually dominant arrangement defines the kind of balance a piece employs. Quilt artist Ruth McDowell, who wrote the book on symmetry for quilters, agrees—in a visual arena, visual trumps structural!

Additional Design Exercise

Paper collage is a way to practice balance without feeling the pressure of wasting precious fabric.

1. From old magazines, tear out pieces of colored and black-and-white paper in different sizes and shapes.

2. Working quickly and intuitively, glue pieces of the paper to a piece of 8½″ × 11″ white paper or a sketchbook page. Make a design using symmetrical balance of some kind.

3. Continue making these symmetrical collages until you have done 20–30.

4. Now do 20–30 collages that are asymmetrically balanced.

5. Select 3–5 of the symmetrical collages and 3–5 of the asymmetrical ones that you think are the most successful designs.

6. Try to articulate why the designs are successful.

Creativity Exercise

Balance is not just a visual principle; when you feel balanced and centered you can access your creative "juice" most easily.

Have someone take a picture of you in your studio space. Below the picture write a positive statement about your ability to work when you feel in touch with your creative center, such as, "I do my best when I stop worrying about outcome."

Suggested Reading

Aimone, Steven. *Design! A Lively Guide to Design Basics for Artists and Craftspeople.* New York: Sterling Publishing Co., 2004.

Bang, Molly. *Picture This: How Pictures Work.* New York: SeaStar Books, 2000.

Bevlin, Marjorie Elliott. *Design through Discovery: An Introduction to Art and Design.* 5th ed. New York: Harcourt Brace Jovanovich College Publishers, 1989.

Elam, Kimberly. *Geometry of Design.* New York: Princeton Architectural Press, 2001.

McDowell, Ruth. *Symmetry: A Design System for Quiltmakers.* Lafayette, CA: C&T Publishing, 1994. (Available as an electronic download at www.ctpub.com.)

Asymmetrical Composition and Value

Asymmetrical balance is the hardest type of balance to master. As you learned in the first exercise, symmetry, by its nature, is balanced. Asymmetry, in contrast, can be balanced or not balanced, depending on your arrangement.

Lorraine's college drawing professor would project slides of asymmetrical master paintings on a screen, put them out of focus, and ask the students to draw the basic structure of the composition as a value study. The instructor's aim was to show that there was a well-balanced structure to these old paintings apart from any details or subject matter. By drawing these structures, the students began to internalize good composition unconsciously. They began to see the visual weight of the different values and how they were dispersed on the picture plane. They noticed that their eyes connected the blurry shapes of the same value, and traveled from one to another in a path. There was a sense of evenness in visual weight, rather than the sameness of a symmetrically balanced composition.

Lorraine has used this same teaching tool in her design classes for quilters, but instead of having them extract the basic composition in charcoal on paper, they are asked to cut out and fuse, glue, or baste fabric scraps in various values (color is optional) to a foundation. From this process, the students can study and understand different successful asymmetrical compositions and develop their own intuition for this type of balance. The following assignment uses just 3 master paintings instead of the 24 from which design students usually choose in Lorraine's class.

the assignment

Refer to the Introduction (page 7) for construction options.

From the three master paintings provided, distill the basic structure or composition based on the values and shapes. Try not to be influenced by details or subject matter. Interpret the compositions in fabric using colored or black, white, and gray fabrics. As always, you may fuse, glue, or baste your fabric sketches. The goals of the exercises are

- to copy, and thereby learn about, good asymmetrical composition;

- to identify value as you choose fabrics that are the same values used in the paintings; and

- to learn to sketch in fabric, trying out ideas quickly to make an idea visual.

Here are black-and-white images of three master paintings to sketch in fabric:

Georges Seurat, French, 1859–1891, *A Sunday Afternoon on La Grande Jatte – 1884,* 1884–86, Oil on canvas, 81¾″ × 121¼″ (207.5cm × 308.1cm), Helen Birch Bartlett Memorial Collection, 1926.224, The Art Institute of Chicago. Photography © The Art Institute of Chicago.

Johannes Vermeer, Dutch, 1632–1675. *A Young Woman Standing at a Virginal,* 1670–72. Reproduced by courtesy of the National Gallery, London. Photography © The National Gallery 2008.

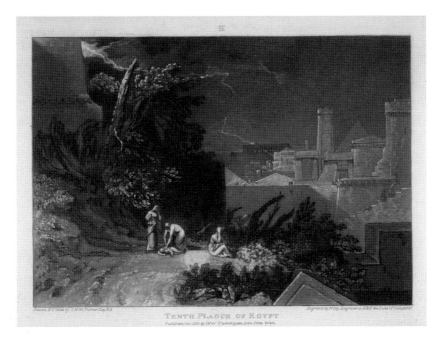

William Turner, English, 1775–1851, *The Tenth Plague of Egypt,* 1802, Etching. Reproduced by courtesy of the Fitzwilliam Museum, Cambridge. Photography © The Fitzwilliam Museum.

JANE worked quickly and tried to concentrate on the most important lights and darks rather than all the shades in between. She says this was a hard assignment for her because it was difficult to choose only the most important, defining shapes and values. She was dissatisfied with the exercises in the end and welcomed the critiques of the others to help her understand how she could have done them better.

" Jane's decision to work in just black, white, and grays allowed her to concentrate on value alone in interpreting these works."
– Abbi

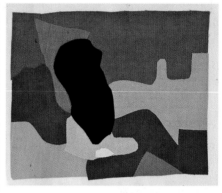

Turner The group thought Jane's abstracted Turner was a well-balanced generalization of the original. Most felt that the light area depicting the city was lighter than the total area in the etching but that the balance in value was maintained in a similar proportion to the original.

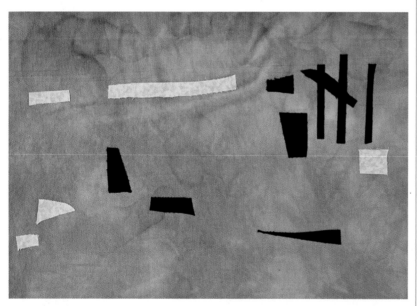

Seurat In interpreting the complex Seurat, with all its small and scattered shapes in a full range of values, Jane chose a minimalist style, reducing everything to a few lines and wedges. Several thought the uniformity of the value in Jane's gray background did not represent the three horizontal layers they saw behind all the details of the original painting. Most thought the dark and light fragments were not as well balanced as those in the painting; by using more darks in the lower left and more lights in the upper right corner, Jane could have maintained a similar balance to the original. Lorraine thought that cropping the four sides of the background, so the shapes would not float so much, would help balance the composition.

Vermeer This time it was Ruth, Marj, and Bonny who suggested that Jane crop her Vermeer abstraction at the top and bottom to achieve a more balanced composition, and Lorraine agreed. Several thought that in order to maintain the balance of the original, the virginal figure should have been a darker, more dominant value and should have extended to the right and bottom edges of the picture plane.

MARJ used two different assembly techniques in her assignment. Two exercises are fused organic shapes that retain many of the paintings' details. The third exercise, the Vermeer, uses topstitched squares and triangles, taking advantage of the geometric shapes in the composition to capture the essence of the painting. Marj agreed with Jane that the Seurat was especially difficult to reduce to its essence, because of the complexity of the many small pieces.

Vermeer Everyone thought Marj's use of traditional shapes to interpret the strong angles and spaces of the Vermeer worked very well. Lorraine and Jane thought Marj was successful in letting her own sense of composition dictate the variations she added while still maintaining the balance created by Vermeer. They noted in particular the reduction of the bottom right corner of the painting to a light triangle, the generalization of the lower left of the painting to an all-dark area, and, in an especially endearing touch, the change of the smaller painting on the wall to a square on point, echoing the diagonals in her abstraction.

Seurat Ruth felt that Marj's Seurat captured the spirit of the original painting quite well, but Sharon thought there were a few value relationships that Marj missed. She thought that to provide more balance, the umbrella in the right foreground should have been a dark value and that additional dark elements should have been used at the lower left corner—perhaps on a more medium-valued background across the bottom. Amalia liked the detail and thought the use of color was successful.

Turner Marj's interpretation of the Turner was viewed by most of the group as successful in mimicking the asymmetrical composition and the stormy, turbulent feel of the etching. Marj kept the city area lighter than that area in the original but, as Jane did, maintained the balance of the composition.

RUTH says she learned a lot about the distribution of value and the variety of shapes she could use. She thought the variety of patterned fabric she chose may have been distracting.

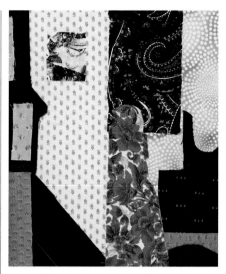

Seurat Most of the group felt that Ruth's use of the three horizontal value bands as a foundation, combined with multicolored fabric that generalized the detail in the Seurat painting, was a successful abstraction of its structure. Several found the printed fabric a bit too busy and inaccurate in value to faithfully sum up the asymmetrical balance in the composition.

Turner Ruth's organic fabric sketch of the Turner depicted the composition successfully. There were a few minor points discussed about some of the values Ruth used in her details: Sharon thought the light V in the upper left was lighter than depicted in the etching, Abbi observed that the light organic shape at center left was lighter than the light shown on the bush, and Marj thought the feeling of the abstraction was different from the original. Perhaps the striped ikat-patterned fabric used for the sky did not represent the stormy sky well enough? But all qualified their comments by saying that these observations were minor.

Vermeer Everyone agreed that Ruth's Vermeer was true to the composition of the original. There was some disagreement, however. Half the group liked the use of the particular prints in the woman's dress and the large painting to capture the value changes in the subjects, but the other half thought the prints chosen were distracting, too dominant, and of the wrong scale to accurately represent the balance in the original work. Sharon and Lorraine thought the straight line down the center of the composition, comprised of the edge of the painting and the back of the woman's dress, should have been a softer and less distracting value to better match its counterpart in the original painting.

> " Contrary to how Ruth felt, I think the choice of patterned fabrics to represent the notion of detail in the original works makes Ruth's exercises effective."
> – Bonny

SHARON, like Jane, limited herself to black, white, and gray fabrics to study the compositions of the master paintings. Her goal was to discover the essence of the paintings in values. She abstracted the images so she could strip out just the dark or light values, independent of what the images represented. It was a challenge to overcome the urge to add more and include minutia. Abstraction is a challenge for Sharon, so this was good practice.

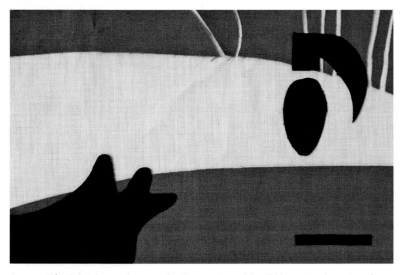

Seurat "If I didn't know this was the Seurat, I would still like it. But knowing that it is a study of the Seurat, my eye fills in the missing details. It is so minimalist and graphic," said Bonny. Amalia was surprised at how little it took to capture the structure and balance of the composition. Cindy thought Sharon used good judgment in not adding too much information and still keeping the work balanced. Marj and Bonny both wanted a bit more detail, perhaps in the form of a subtly patterned gray fabric across the middle to capture the busyness in the original, or a few small dark pieces in the center left side.

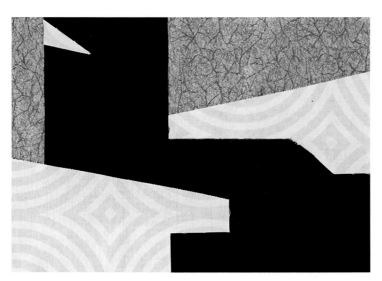

Turner The overall reaction of the group to Sharon's simple, cut-to-the-chase abstractions—but particularly to the Turner—was amazement that this was all she really needed to capture the essence of the composition. Some felt that a textured gray for the city area might have better represented the changes in value.

> ❝ Sharon truly distilled the important elements down to the simplest form." – Jane

Vermeer There was widespread agreement that Sharon had found the essence of the original painting in her depiction of the Vermeer. The only disagreement was regarding the fabric chosen for the dress of the woman. Most thought the high-contrast striped fabric worked well, but Abbi felt the values were more stark and high contrast in this piece than in the figure in the painting. Bonny thought that repeating the white in a small amount somewhere else in the sketch would have helped distribute the values more accurately and would have softened the dominance of the sole black-and-white area.

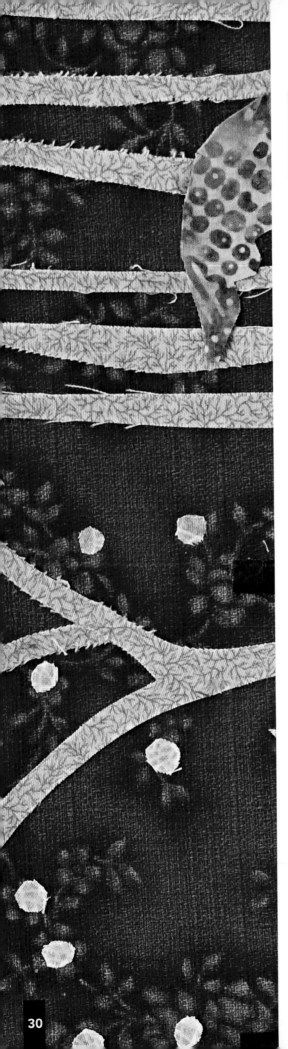

the continuing education process

In studying value in any composition, whether it is one you are trying to abstract or one you are building on your design wall, it is helpful to know how to determine the value of a color. Following are some tools for reading value:

- Squint. Squinting allows you to more easily break down a piece into the most general values. When you squint, your eyelashes come together and block out light. Since light is what enables you to see color, color is taken out of the equation, and what is left is value.

- Get distance on your work. Getting away from your work allows you to see the piece without the detail that closeness provides. Distance also diminishes the perception of color, which leaves a clearer reading of the value.

- Use a device that simulates getting distance from your work. A reducing glass, a camera viewfinder, the wrong end of binoculars, or a door peephole all work to create a small and seemingly distant view of your work.

- Consider a value finder. Red or green Plexiglas value finders work well to translate everything into one color with different values. The problem with these tools is that they read their own color inaccurately: Red, seen through the red Plexiglas, is white or much lighter than it actually is. Green, seen through green, is also too light. Lorraine's preference is not to use these tools if she has to qualify what she sees with them.

- Dim the lights. Turn down the lights in the room or look at your work at dawn or dusk without the lights on.

Additional Design Exercise

1. Cut the following from black construction paper or fabric:

1 square 2½″ × 2½″

1 square 1½″ × 1½″

1 square 1″ × 1″

1 square ¾″ × ¾″

1 square ½″ × ½″

2. Arrange these squares on a piece of 8½″ × 11″ white paper so the arrangement is asymmetrically balanced. Record the arrangement in a sketch, scan, or photograph.

3. Continue trying different asymmetrical arrangements, recording each as you proceed. In some, try abutting the squares or even overlapping them. Try letting some of the squares go off the edge of the paper. Try placing some of them diagonally.

4. Compare your examples. Are there some that are better than others? Can you identify why? Notice the spacing between squares, the closeness to the edge, and the distance to the vertical centerline of the background paper. Keep thinking about the teeter-totter and the proximity of the shapes to the fulcrum (balance point), or the centerline of the background paper.

5. Expand your exercise by changing the numbers, sizes, shapes, and colors of the pieces that you cut out to place on the background. Change the background color.

Think about using one of these compositions as the skeleton of a quilt design. Or actually re-create it in a fabric composition.

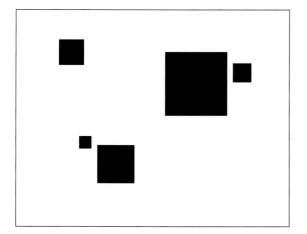

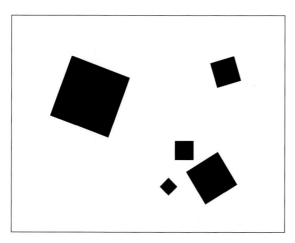

Creativity Exercise

Call a friend. Make a date to go to a gallery or museum. Exposure to art in galleries and museums is important in keeping your own creativity primed. Pay particular attention to balance, composition, and color in the work you observe. Committing to doing this with another person will help make it happen. Make a list of places you want to go and check them off as you visit them.

Suggested Reading

Kent, Sarah. *Composition*. London: Dorling Kindersley, 1995.

Ocvirk, Otto G., Robert E. Stinson, Philip R. Wigg, Robert O. Bone, and David L. Clayton. *Art Fundamentals: Theory and Practice*. Boston: McGraw-Hill, 1998.

Poore, Henry Rankin. *Pictorial Composition: An Introduction (Composition in Art)*. New York: Dover Publications, 1976. (Originally published in 1967 by Sterling Publishing Co.)

Scale, Value, and Balance

Most quilters already understand the value of varying the scale of the printed fabrics they combine in a quilt. If all the fabrics are big, random, dense prints, the quilt could look confusing or too busy. If all the fabrics are small, regular, open prints, the quilt probably will be boring and visually flat. But another way you must understand the effects of scale is in terms of the relative sizes of the pieces in a quilt. Most good compositions have balanced arrangements of large spaces, medium spaces, and small spaces.

This exercise will show you the importance of varying the scale in your quilts. At the same time, you will practice identifying the value of colored fabric and reinforce your skills in balancing your work.

the assignment

What You'll Need

- ¹⁄₄ yard (or fat quarter) each of 5 different fabrics—
  1 each of light, medium-light, medium, medium-dark, and dark values

  Choose any color of fabrics you like; however, each fabric must represent 1 of the 5 light to dark values relative to the other selected fabrics.

- 3 foundation squares 16″ × 16″

- 2¹⁄₄ yards paper-backed fusible web, 17″ wide (optional)

  Use muslin for the foundation and paper-backed fusible web to adhere the shapes, or use fusible interfacing for the foundation and fuse the shapes directly to the interfacing.

- Pressing sheet or parchment paper

Monochromatic

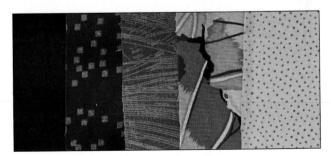

Multicolored

Your five values of fabric can be monochromatic (one color) or multicolored (see Exercise 5 on color, pages 44–51).

Instructions

Refer to the Introduction (page 7) for construction options.

1. Cut the following from the selected fabrics.

Dark	Medium-dark	Medium	Medium-light	Light
3 squares 8″ × 8″	6 squares 4″ × 4″	6 squares 4″ × 4″	6 squares 4″ × 4″	6 squares 4″ × 4″
9 squares 2″ × 2″	12 squares 1″ × 1″	9 squares 2″ × 2″	12 squares 1″ × 1″	9 squares 2″ × 2″
12 squares 1″ × 1″	9 squares ½″ × ½″	12 squares 1″ × 1″	9 squares ½″ × ½″	12 squares 1″ × 1″
12 squares ½″ × ½″		9 squares ½″ × ½″		9 squares ½″ × ½″
12 rectangles ½″ × 2″				

2. Divide the cut shapes into 3 identical piles. In each pile of fabrics, all the pieces will fit together to make a 16″ block. Each pile should contain the following:

Dark	Medium-dark	Medium	Medium-light	Light
1 square 8″ × 8″	2 squares 4″ × 4″	2 squares 4″ × 4″	2 squares 4″ × 4″	2 squares 4″ × 4″
3 squares 2″ × 2″	4 squares 1″ × 1″	3 squares 2″ × 2″	4 squares 1″ × 1″	3 squares 2″ × 2″
4 squares 1″ × 1″	3 squares ½″ × ½″	4 squares 1″ × 1″	3 squares ½″ × ½″	4 squares 1″ × 1″
4 squares ½″ × ½″		3 squares ½″ × ½″		3 squares ½″ × ½″
4 rectangles ½″ × 2″				

3. Arrange all the shapes in one pile on one of the foundation squares to make a 16″ × 16″ square block using some kind of **symmetry** (see page 17). Use the shapes in the 2 other piles and the remaining foundations to make 2 **asymmetrical** blocks.

4. Cover each block with a pressing sheet or parchment paper and fuse the shapes, following the manufacturer's directions, to finalize the designs.

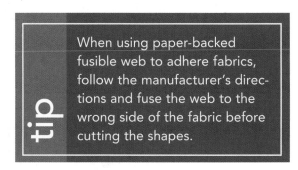

tip

When using paper-backed fusible web to adhere fabrics, follow the manufacturer's directions and fuse the web to the wrong side of the fabric before cutting the shapes.

BONNY chose a monochromatic group of fabrics for her exercises. She combined red in three values with two values of gray, resulting in five distinct values. The visual texture and scale of all of Bonny's fabrics is similar—mottled, rather than different sizes of prints. Some of the students thought this added more visual unity. Others thought the similarity in the scale of the fabrics made it even more important to vary the scale of the sizes of the pieces. Everyone agreed that the small pieces added interest, sparkle, and balance to the compositions.

Asymmetrical Bonny found the 8″ dark square very challenging to work into a 16″ asymmetrical composition. But everyone agreed that the clustering of the small pieces gave the composition enough visual activity to balance the large, heavy, dark shape on the lower right.

Symmetrical For Bonny, the most obvious way to make a symmetrical composition, with the mixture of sizes and values assigned, was to place her arrangement on point. As a scientist, Bonny was not satisfied to make a composition that was almost symmetrical; it had to be exactly symmetrical. So, with many of the shapes in sets of three, placing the piece on point was her solution.

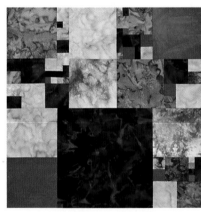

Asymmetrical In this asymmetrical composition, the dark square on the bottom has plenty of competition in the upper half of the block to balance it. The bright red 4″ squares and the relative busyness of the splotchy medium-dark 4″ square toward the right in the second row provide balance for the large dark square.

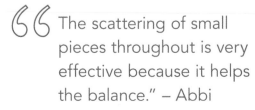

" The scattering of small pieces throughout is very effective because it helps the balance." – Abbi

ABBI'S exercises have a strong graphic feel, largely due to the high value contrast in the blocks. The light and medium-light she chose were close enough in value to be considered both lights. The dark and medium-dark were actually both darks, resulting in three values instead of five. Abbi had picked all the fabrics from her stash, and this analysis of her selections made her realize that she didn't have a good value range from which to choose. In spite of this, the group liked her compositions and found them balanced and dynamic.

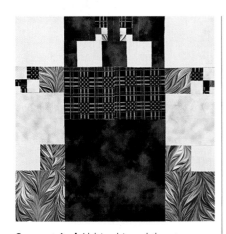

Symmetrical Abbi achieved the strong architectural feel in her symmetrical composition by combining nearly all the darks into one monolithic center shape with windows of light. She connected so many of the small pieces to make larger ones that this piece doesn't have the sparkle that the small shapes in Bonny's piece provide (page 34), but the few small pieces, as well as the variety of scale in the printed fabric, add enough visual texture and activity to create a successful design.

Asymmetrical Carefully placed mediums and darks balance this asymmetrical composition. Compared to Abbi's previous block, the more visible small pieces add movement in the strong, dramatic arrangement.

Symmetrical variation Abbi conceived this block with the right side as the top, describing it as kind of symmetrical but with some variation. On its side, it is both asymmetrical and balanced. The concentration of the medium-value marbled fabric, as well as the small squares on the right half of the block, adds enough visual weight to balance the large dark square.

Although the assignment was to identify and use five distinct values, Abbi's three-value compositions were dramatic and successful. Even though it is usually worthwhile to learn what you can from following an assignment, **not** following it can often produce wonderful results **and** teach you something. The key is to recognize that you are departing from the assignment and to know why you are doing it!

66 Most of us had a hard time using the 8″ dark square because it was so big. But Abbi positioned many of the smaller dark pieces so they enlarged the 8″ square, making it even bigger. She successfully created new shapes by joining pieces of the same fabric!" – Jane

MARJ surprised everyone by doing two things that were not part of the assignment: fusing her shapes to a brightly colored foundation, letting some of it show, and cutting some of her shapes into other shapes. Cindy remarked that Marj's compositions had more of an organic feel than many of the others. The liveliness and movement she noticed was a result of the combination of prints and the less-than-exact placement of the pieces on the foundation.

Symmetrical variation Marj's desire to break up the big dark square compelled her to cut it into four pieces, allowing the bright pink foundation to show. She admits she had to fudge a bit by trimming the pieces to slightly smaller dimensions to make everything fit in the 16″ square. This block has the appearance of symmetry, even though technically it is not symmetrical.

Asymmetrical This asymmetrical block is balanced because the smaller pieces of the black fabric are positioned from roughly the center to the left, balancing the large dark area on the lower right. Abbi noted that clusters of small pieces create enough activity and visual weight to balance a large, heavy, dark area.

Asymmetrical To achieve this mixture of straight-set pieces and diagonally set pieces in this asymmetrical arrangement, Marj cut some of the squares into triangles to fill in the spaces. Cutting the large dark square into a $1/3$-to-$2/3$ proportion is unexpected and effective. The thin bright pink lines between some of the pieces enhance the variety of scale in the block. They also help separate some of the busy fabrics. Marj likes this one best!

❝ The pink lines used in some places produce a lot of motion. Marj also added a lot of sparkle with the choice of fabrics—both the large-scale flower print and the more linear birch tree print. She's got a lot of little spaces in those fabrics." – Bonny

the continuing education process

In the exercise, you saw the importance of **varying the scale** in your work. You can accomplish this goal by doing any or all of the following:

- Varying the scale of the printed fabric

- Varying the sizes of the pieces

- Creating larger pieces to contrast with medium-sized and smaller ones by combining pieces of similar-value fabrics

In some of the exercises, you saw that higher contrast provides more emphasis to even a few small pieces.

You also practiced **determining the value of a color** when you selected five different values for these pieces. Those who kept to a monochromatic color scheme found the selection of five values easier. Those who chose a multicolored group of fabrics got more practice identifying the relative values of colors. Some selected a wide value range and others chose a close value range. But in every case there was enough contrast to see the design. Remember that **value defines a composition**. You must have at least a little contrast to read the design of the piece. High contrast or low contrast is a matter of personal taste, or your goal for the piece, but **no contrast** usually means mush.

Even in these abstract, geometric pieces, you can **try out different kinds of balance**. Without balance of some kind, a composition is dissatisfying because it doesn't make visual sense.

Once again, trying out your ideas quickly helps you audition fabric and visual ideas. Sketching in fabric is not a waste of fabric or time. It equates to batting practice for a baseball player, or playing scales for a pianist. Practice is as essential to quilters and fiber artists as it is to athletes and musicians!

Additional Design Exercise

The following is another simple exercise to reinforce the lesson that variety of scale is important.

1. Select 6 different colors of paper or fabric.

2. From each of the 6 colors, cut out 1 square 3″ × 3″.

3. Glue the squares edge to edge in a 2-across-by-3-down arrangement in the center of a piece of 8½″ × 11″ white paper.

4. Assuming this represents a little quilt, ask yourself if it is very interesting. Most of you would probably answer, "Not very."

5. Now add a border of smaller pieces of the same 6 colors. You may find that it is possible to balance an otherwise unbalanced arrangement of color and value in the original little quilt with your positioning of the colors in the border.

6. Try the exercise again by adding the smaller-scale pieces to the inside of the little quilt instead of to the border.

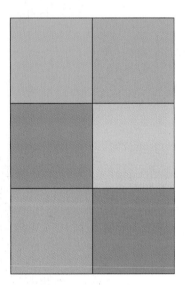

A small quilt with no scale variation

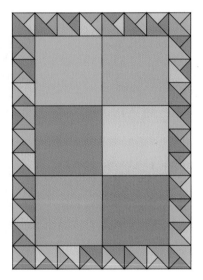

Scale variation added in a border

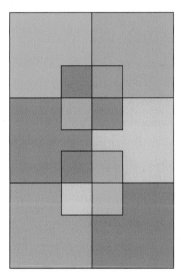

Scale variation added in the interior of the quilt

Don't you agree that this simple attention to scale variation makes a big, and positive, difference?

Creativity Exercise

Find music that inspires, affirms, and energizes you. Play it in your studio. Breathe quietly and listen before you begin your work. See where the music takes you and your work. Different rhythms, volume levels, styles, and so on can inspire different outcomes in your work. Make a list of types of music that are particularly good for you when you are creating.

Suggested Reading

Dantzic, Cynthia Maris. *Design Dimensions: An Introduction to the Visual Surface.* Englewood Cliffs, NJ: Prentice Hall, 1990.

Edwards, Betty. *Drawing on the Artist Within.* New York: Simon & Schuster, 1986.

Johnston, Ann. *The Quilter's Book of Design.* Chicago: Quilt Digest Press, 2000.

McNiff, Shaun. *Trust the Process: An Artist's Guide to Letting Go.* Boston: Shambhala Publications, 1998.

Wong, Wucius. *Principles of Form and Design.* New York: Van Nostrand Reinhold, 1993.

Identifying Value in Color

Value, or the lightness or darkness of a color, is one of the most important considerations in designing any quilt. Every color can be presented in an infinite range of value. If you add white to a color, the result is said to be a **tint** of the color. If you add black to a color, you will have a **shade** of the color. Varying the value in your quilt is, after all, what defines its composition. You can choose high or low value contrast, but without at least **some** contrast in your quilt, you will not be able to read the composition. The perceived value of a color is relative to the values of the colors that surround it.

Much of what determines the balance in a piece is the distribution of darks, mediums, and lights. Of course, the challenge is determining the values of the colored fabrics you are using in your quilt. Review the tips on identifying value in color on page 30.

In this value exercise, you will start with a simple achromatic (meaning without color: comprised of only black, white, and their combination, gray) composition. You will add color to it in two different ways to replicate the values in the achromatic composition, and then change it in two different ways.

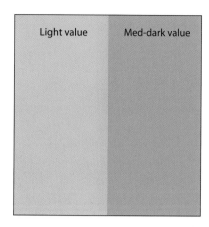

High value contrast

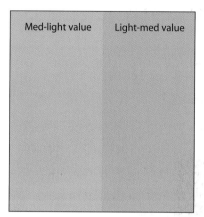

Low value contrast

Refer to the Introduction (page 7) for construction options.

the assignment

1. Design a balanced achromatic composition in black, white, and gray.

2. Repeat the composition, substituting colors for the blacks, whites, and grays of the first composition, but keeping the values the same as those in the original.

3. Repeat the composition a second time, changing the colors again but keeping the values the same as those in the original composition.

4. Repeat the composition again, but change the colors this time so the values are different from those in the original composition and balanced differently.

5. Repeat the composition one final time, this time changing the colors so the values are different from those in the original composition and are **not** balanced.

ABBI chose a simple four-block symmetrical composition of concentric squares of two colorings. She says she ran into difficulty trying to come up with an out-of-balance composition for the last part of the assignment. (Not a bad problem to have!)

" Abbi did a great job of creating a very different balance in her fourth exercise by using the red centers and very close values throughout the rest of the block." – Jane

Achromatic (1) Abbi's balanced design is an effective black-and-white arrangement of concentric squares. The visual texture of so many different fabrics adds interest.

Changing colors while maintaining values (2) Although the pink squares within the larger dark squares read lighter than their corresponding squares in the achromatic block, the overall composition is quite similar to the original.

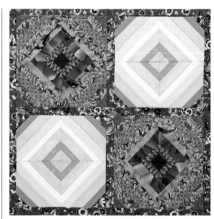

Changing colors while maintaining values (3) As in the previous block, the orange squares in the dark quadrants seem lighter and brighter than the corresponding squares in the original achromatic composition.

Changing colors, values, and balance (4) Everyone liked this glowing close-value arrangement showing balance in a different value arrangement.

Changing colors and values and removing balance (5) Everyone agreed that Abbi's unbalanced composition was actually balanced, and in much the same way the original block was balanced. Suggestions to make it unbalanced included randomly coloring some sides of the squares in different values, coloring three squares light and one dark, or placing two light squares on one side and two dark squares on the other.

AMALIA used a traditional block to practice her value placement. She, like Abbi, discovered that having a wide value range in her stash in all colors would have made this assignment easier. She was surprised to learn that she usually thinks of a color as being a certain value—for example, she thinks of yellow as light and green as dark. She was reminded that any color can be any value with the addition of black or white. A broad value and color range in your stash usually helps in the creation of all quilts!

Achromatic (1) This strong, well-balanced block in black, white, and gray is a good start for Amalia's exercises.

Changing colors while maintaining values (2) There was widespread agreement that this colored version of the original block was similar in value placement but that the smallest dark squares contrasted with the green background square more than those two areas contrasted in the achromatic square.

Changing colors while maintaining values (3) This square matches the previous one very well in value placement but with a different color palette. It departs from the value placement of the original in the same way the second square does. Amalia confessed that she had confined herself to fabrics she had in her stash rather than buying more fabric.

Changing colors, values, and balance (4) Amalia transformed her square into a Snail's Trail block with the simple device of changing the values of some of her colors. Even though the values are positioned differently in this block, it is certainly balanced.

Changing colors and values and removing balance (5) Amalia's unbalanced piece struck everyone as meeting the requirement of the assignment. The placement of the heavy, dark fabric in the upper left definitely creates a left-heavy square. Lorraine thought the medium violet in the lower right was almost heavy enough to create an asymmetrically balanced piece.

> " This set of blocks is a fabulous example of the power of value and color placement to achieve new looks."
> – Jane

RUTH designed this block to have asymmetrical balance. The eleven pieces in the block allowed her to repeat most of the values in more than one position so she could achieve a good distribution of visual weight. She and Abbi agreed that the introduction of color increased the difficulty of identifying and correctly placing the values in the blocks that were to mimic the original block.

Achromatic (1) Ruth's achromatic design is a well-defined composition with balance and clarity. The solids of the achromatic piece help convey this clarity. Jane felt that the addition of color and pattern in subsequent pieces actually detracted from the beautiful simplicity of the design.

Changing colors while maintaining values (2) With the addition of color in this piece, Ruth maintained roughly the same balance as in the achromatic piece. Abbi suggested that the values would be more closely represented if the fabrics in the two dark shapes in the bottom center and right were reversed.

Changing colors while maintaining values (3) This third block still simulates the value placement of the original block, but as Sharon noted, the batiks in the middle values bleed together a bit more than in the black, white, and gray piece.

Changing colors, values, and balance (4) Ruth changed the value placement in this piece but kept it balanced. Cindy thought it was more effective because of the way the greens and yellows were balanced in the midst of the darker reds and blacks, but Marj thought the composition would be more effective if the colors did not contrast as much and were more connected.

Changing colors and values and removing balance (5) Ruth said she found it hard to create a deliberately unbalanced block. Others agreed that it was hard, but most thought this block was, indeed, unbalanced. Lorraine thought that with a few more dark values in the center bottom, Ruth would have another differently balanced block.

66 While lacking the tension of the first three, her differently balanced block is also successful." – Abbi

the continuing education process

Remember that the value of color is relative. A color that is a medium value when you are considering the whole value range from white to black may appear dark if all the other colors in your quilt are light. Conversely, the same medium may be perceived as light if all the other colors on your quilt are dark. Shapes of similar value can also be used to balance a quilt. Our eyes tend to search for, and connect, **similar** elements in a composition. Repeated values, as shapes or objects, become connected by our eyes, helping to unify and balance a composition if the shapes are places in a balanced arrangement relative to the center line in the composition.

Additional Design Exercise

The following exercise will give you more practice in identifying the values of colors.

1. Collect as many pieces of colored paper in as many different colors and values as you can.

2. Cut the paper into pieces roughly 1″ × 2″.

3. Cut a piece of 8½″ × 11″ white paper in half lengthwise. Tape it together end to end.

4. Arrange the colored paper pieces on the white background by value, starting with the lightest piece and ending with the darkest piece. Place the pieces edge to edge so that no white paper shows between the pieces, interfering with proper comparison. After you have arranged, and perhaps rearranged, the pieces to your satisfaction, glue or tape them down.

5. Dim the lights in the room, or use one of the value perception methods described on page 30. How did you do at identifying the values of the colors? This is not easy, so don't be discouraged if it takes a few attempts. You will notice that there are several exercises in this book that contain lessons on value. You can't practice this too much.

Creativity Exercise

Find and observe a surface (for example, brick), object (for example, a stone), flower, tree (leaves or bark), or animal. Look closely. Count how many different values of color you can discern in what you originally saw to be one color.

Suggested Reading

Bothwell, Dorr, and Marlys Mayfield. *Notan: The Dark-Light Principle of Design.* New York: Dover Publications, 1991.

Dow, Arthur Wesley. *Composition: Understanding Line, Notan and Color.* Berkeley, CA: University of California Press, 1997. (Republication of 1920 13th edition by Doubleday.)

Lauer, David A., and Stephen Pentak. *Design Basics.* 6th ed. Belmont, CA: Wadsworth/Thompson Learning, 2005.

Do you see places where the colors could be rearranged to accomplish a smoother value gradation?

Color

The first thing most people notice about any quilt is its color. Most of us react emotionally to color and have very subjective, personal preferences. Our first exercises in color will be ones that simply try out different traditional color schemes so that you can identify them and begin to develop an appreciation for colors and color combinations other than your usual preferences. The process should give you insight into what makes you like or dislike a color or group of colors.

There are many different theories and organizations of color, and different color wheels—a study of which would be very lengthy, academic, and, perhaps, without conclusive evidence of which is correct. For our purposes, we will confine ourselves to using a twelve-part color wheel that has three primary colors: red, yellow, and blue. Mixing two primary colors together produces the color wheel's secondary colors: green, orange, and violet. Tertiary colors on the color wheel are produced by mixing a primary color with its neighboring secondary color. Tertiary colors are yellow-green, blue-green, blue-violet, red-violet, red-orange, and yellow-orange.

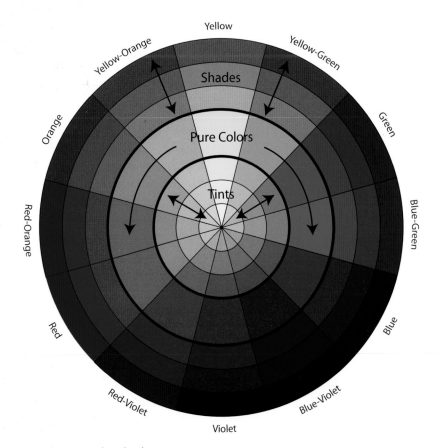

Black and white and gray are achromatic (page 39) and lack color or hue. Adding black, white, or gray to a color does not change its **hue**, only its value. A color with white added is a **tint** of that color. A color with black added is a **shade** of that color. A color with gray (black + white) added is a **tone** of that color. Tints, shades, and tones of a color still qualify as that color. If you have ever been to a paint store to have a color mixed, you know that an infinite number of colors can be made mixing a pure color with other colors from the color wheel.

A twelve-part color wheel

Refer to the Introduction (page 7) for construction options.

1. Design a simple, well-balanced composition as a line drawing.

2. Interpret the composition with an **achromatic** color scheme.

Achromatic color scheme—no color: black, white, and/or gray

3. Interpret that same composition as a **monochromatic** color scheme.

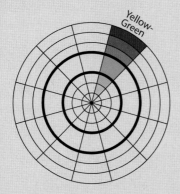

Monochromatic color scheme—one color only, in any of its values (the pure color, its shades, and/or its tints) plus black, white, and/or gray, if you wish

4. Interpret that same composition as an **analogous** color scheme.

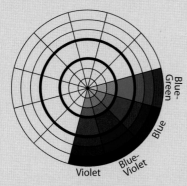

Analogous color scheme—colors next to each other on the color wheel; usually 3 to 4 colors

5. Interpret the same composition as a **complementary** color scheme or some variation of complementary: **split-complementary** or **double split-complementary.**

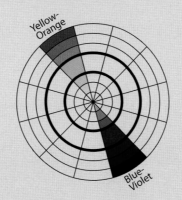

Complementary color scheme—colors opposite each other on the color wheel

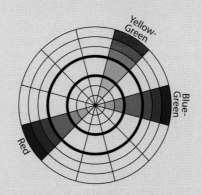

Split-complementary color scheme—a color and the two colors adjacent to its complement

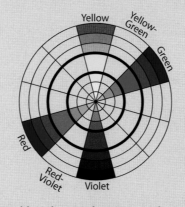

Double split-complementary color scheme—the two colors on either side of a color (such as yellow-green) and the two colors on either side of the color's complement (in this case red-violet)

6. Interpret the same composition as a **triadic** color scheme.

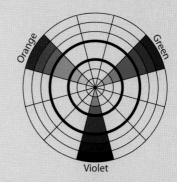

Triadic color scheme—colors dividing the color wheel into thirds

7. Interpret the same composition as a **polychromatic** color scheme.

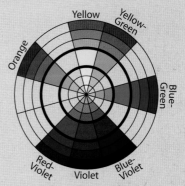

Polychromatic color scheme—all or many colors: a combination that exceeds the limited number of colors recognized as fitting within other color schemes

8. Optional: Interpret the same composition using a **tetradic** color scheme.

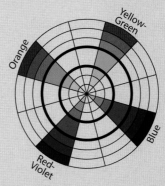

Tetradic color scheme—colors dividing the color wheel into fourths

the critique session

BONNY wanted a simple composition in which she could not only try out the color schemes but play with the illusion of transparency as well. The large overlapping squares she used in her design are actually a combination of smaller shapes, which enabled her to piece the little compositions. The favorites of different members of the group reflected individual color preferences and reactions to features other than color, such as the visual texture of the prints and the illusion of transparency.

Achromatic color scheme Bonny's achromatic piece, in blacks, whites, and grays, successfully represents the color scheme, but everyone also thought it worked equally well to show the illusion of transparency.

Monochromatic color scheme The accurately represented monochromatic color scheme uses green in various tints, shades, and tones. Even the background is a very pale tint of green.

Analogous color scheme The yellow, yellow-orange, orange, red-orange, and red of this analogous piece has a very successful illusion of transparency. Ruth and Jane pointed out that the blue background stepped outside the boundaries of an analogous color scheme, which normally is restricted to about four adjacent colors.

Complementary color scheme Yellow-green, violet, and red make up this split-complementary color scheme. While most of the students agreed that the print containing the three colors did not contribute to the illusion of transparency, they liked the change in scale that the print provided.

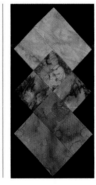

Triadic color scheme This triadic piece is comprised of violet, orange, and green. Abbi thought that to better represent a triadic color scheme, the rather blue-green fabrics should be replaced by a true green. Overall, the group liked the way the mixed color prints in the center squares worked to create the illusion of transparency.

Polychromatic color scheme For Cindy, the colors in this polychromatic design seem to compete rather than harmonize. Jane echoed her feelings by saying, "Polychromatic color schemes are generally harder for viewers to get their minds around, because they are less predictable, less easy to interpret."

Tetradic color scheme Bonny also completed the optional tetradic color scheme exercise. Yellow, violet, blue-green, and red-orange are colors that are appropriate for a tetradic composition because they divide the color wheel into fourths.

66 The image of overlapping boxes sets up an expectation by the viewer that the colors will blend into each other in some way. Adding the challenge of transparency is the perfect relationship device—although I think it only works in her achromatic, analogous, and triadic pieces."
– Sharon

CINDY made her achromatic piece first to define the values in one possibility. Then she could experiment with different value placements in each of the color schemes that followed. She named her pieces *The Many Moods of Mona (Lisa)*. The analogous piece is Cindy's favorite because she introduced more prints for visual texture, and because the close color scheme is very unified.

Achromatic color scheme Cindy's achromatic *Mona* clearly defines the swooping lines of her abstracted woman's head, shoulders, and hair. Bonny thought Cindy was smart to start with the achromatic color scheme as it helped her in choosing the placement of the colors in the other blocks.

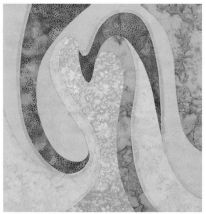

Monochromatic color scheme Cindy chose yellow for her monochromatic color scheme. Most members of the group agreed that this piece was not their favorite because many of the yellows were so close in value that the shapes lost their definition. Also, when people attempt to use many values of yellow, they often use golds for the darker values, not realizing that gold is actually a shade of yellow-orange, not yellow, making the color scheme analogous. (See the color wheel on page 44 for different values of yellow.)

Analogous color scheme This analogous piece was the overwhelming favorite of the group. Not only is Cindy's blue, blue-green, green, and yellow-green piece soothingly coordinated in color, the value placement balances the piece and the visual texture of the batik prints is interestingly varied in scale.

Complementary color scheme
Red-violet and yellow-green are the complements Cindy chose for this piece. Sharon thought the warm red-violet made the cool yellow-green that much crisper. It was one of Bonny's favorites, too, but she felt that it might have benefited from a slightly lighter value of red-violet.

Triadic color scheme Cindy's triadic interpretation in yellow-orange, blue-green, and red-violet showed the richness that colors across and around the color wheel can provide. Abbi thought that the values of the colors, while balanced, began to overtake the lines of the image. Of course, maintaining the reference of the image wasn't a necessity in terms of the assignment—and may not be in your own work.

Polychromatic color scheme In this polychromatic version of *Mona*, Cindy thought the use of so many colors made her forget about value. The addition of the bold print increased the tendency of this piece to be confusing, in Cindy's view. Marj thought that the placement of both of the reds at the bottom interfered with the balance.

MARJ used a traditional star block as the format to try out different color schemes. The border she added to each of the blocks stayed faithful to the color scheme **except** in her achromatic piece. In bordering this piece, she simply couldn't help herself! Amalia liked that the block had the potential to look very different with different color and value placements—and Marj took good advantage of that potential to make different-looking blocks.

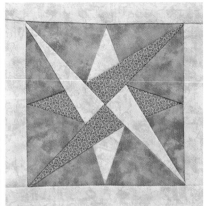

Achromatic color scheme Everyone agreed that the addition of the red border kept this piece from being achromatic, but everyone liked it. There was some disagreement about whether the large-scale background print worked. Bonny thought it was too busy and confused the overall design, while Cindy felt the print made the star vibrate.

Monochromatic color scheme Marj's monochromatic star, like Cindy's block (page 47), is not really monochromatic. She used both yellow and gold (which is actually a shade of yellow-orange) instead of different values of one of these colors. Amalia thought the similarity of values in the background and in the gold star points made the composition suffer a bit, but others liked the use of close values.

Analogous color scheme The great combination of prints and colors in this analogous piece (blue, blue-violet, violet, red-violet) adds to this block's success. Everyone agreed that the block worked from a value standpoint, too. The parts had sufficient contrast to define the design.

> " Marj's stars emphasize that color schemes should be looked on as guidelines and not rules. One can travel further outside the scheme if it makes the design more successful. That red border around the achromatic one looks great—even though it makes it **not** achromatic."
> – Ruth

Complementary color scheme Marj's complementary piece, predominantly in red and green, had the widest border of all the blocks. Cindy thought this worked to contain the energy of the grid and polka dot patterns. Of the five pieces, Bonny liked this one least because she thought the colors looked flat. This might have been because the scale of the prints is smaller in this piece than in the other blocks.

Polychromatic color scheme Marj's polychromatic piece is her favorite. Several others in the group also liked this one because of the lively multicolored background print. The variation in the design that was created by making all the long star points white and the short ones different colors, resembling compass points, was an interesting variation.

SHARON says, "I began with my simple Madonna motif. I found the line created by the negative space as it moved through the composition very appealing. I used my favorite color combinations and fabrics so I found the exercises to be very satisfying. I guess I missed an opportunity to stretch by using colors I don't normally combine." Everyone found Sharon's Madonna motif appealing in its simplicity.

Achromatic color scheme Amalia thought that the simplicity of the shapes and Sharon's use of only two values in most of the pieces let the visual texture of the fabric do a lot of the work. In this achromatic piece, the spirals in the background echo the circular shapes in the motif, providing visual unity.

Monochromatic color scheme This monochromatic piece again relies on visual texture in the black, gray, and red fabrics to enrich it. Bonny felt that most of the backgrounds did not function to improve the pieces.

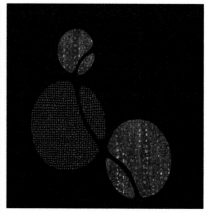

Analogous color scheme The very dark purple (or violet, as it is called in color-wheel terminology) background with the red and red-violet of the motif makes this a limited analogous color scheme. The simplicity of Sharon's motif offered few opportunities to use many colors, said Ruth, so "she was wise to keep her combinations simple too." Cindy thought the dense darkness of this background enveloped the shapes and made the composition more intimate.

Complementary color scheme Sharon's complementary yellow and violet piece made brilliant use of the dotted print containing both colors, Cindy thought. The density of the dots at the bottom of the Madonna figure make it nicely weighted.

Triadic color scheme Abbi thought the subtle values of violet, orange, and green in this triadic color scheme were "almost not colored at all, but still fall within triadic parameters." Jane thought that keeping all the shapes in the motif close in value helped unify the piece.

Polychromatic color scheme Because of the limited opportunity to use many colors, Sharon used multicolored fabric to create a polychromatic color scheme. Cindy said this was her least favorite of the pieces. She said it "needs a background that connects more with the prints and makes a whole composition."

the continuing education process

Most of us do not select our colors so clinically when we pull fabrics to make a quilt. Doing the exercises in this chapter is simply a way to try out color ideas visually to find new combinations that may surprise and excite us. Practicing any discipline also makes us able to use it more intuitively when it really counts.

Additional Design Exercise

Here is another color exercise designed to

- remind you that any color can be any value
- teach you how to better identify value in color
- show you how to recognize what's missing from your stash

tip

Joen Wolfrom's book *Color Play* and her *3-in-1 Color Tool* are good sources for charts showing what each color looks like as it gets darker or lighter.

1. From your stash, select red, yellow, blue, green, orange, and violet fabrics, in as many values as you can find.

2. From your selected fabrics, arrange a gradation of values using red, yellow, blue, green, orange, and violet, in that order. Make the first color, red, the lightest in value, and the last color, violet, the darkest in value. Cut swatches from these fabrics and glue them to a piece of paper in the light-to-dark gradation.

Gradation of values using red, yellow, blue, green, orange, and violet

3. Change the order of the color value gradation using yellow (lightest), orange, red, violet, blue, and green (darkest). Glue these swatches in order on your paper.

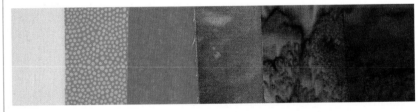

Gradation of values using yellow, orange, red, violet, blue, and green

4. Try it again in this order: green (lightest), blue, violet, orange, red, and yellow (darkest).

Gradation of values using green, blue, violet, orange, red, and yellow. Notice that yellow, with the addition of black to make it darker, looks like what we typically call "olive green." In fact, no blue—or green—has been added to the yellow. This is what dark yellow looks like.

5. Try it again in this order: blue (lightest), violet, orange, yellow, green, and red (darkest).

Gradation of values using blue, violet, orange, yellow, green, and red

Creativity Exercise

Make a list of five colors you avoid or seldom use in your work. On your walks, on trips to galleries or museums, and from observation of others' work, see if you can find places where these colors are used in ways you find pleasing. Take a photo, or record your observation.

Suggested Reading

Feisner, Edith Anderson. *Color Studies*. New York: Fairchild Publications, 2001.

Menz, Deb. *Color Works: The Crafter's Guide to Color*. Loveland, CO: Interweave Press, 2004.

Quiller, Stephen. *Color Choice: Making Color Sense out of Color Theory*. New York: Watson-Guptill Publications, 1989.

Quiller, Stephen. *Painter's Guide to Color*. New York: Watson-Guptill Publications, 1999.

Wolfrom, Joen. *Color Play*. Lafayette, CA: C&T Publishing, 2000.

Wolfrom, Joen. *3-in-1 Color Tool*. Lafayette, CA: C&T Publishing, 2002.

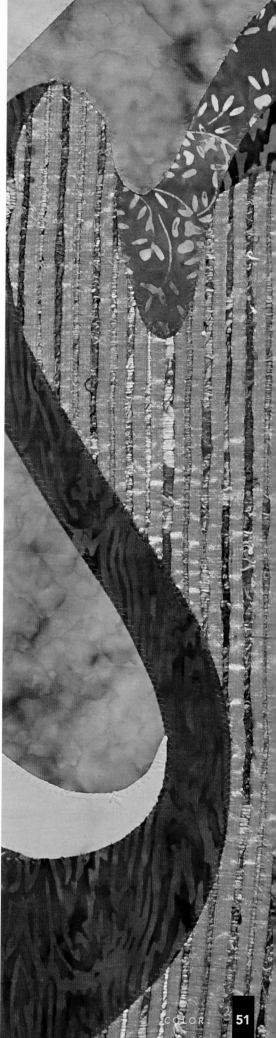

design sources *and* inspiration

In the second part of our design course, the focus is on sources and inspiration; however, the principles and elements of design (starting on page 17) should always remain a part of your consciousness when making design decisions or critiquing your work.

Using Words to Inspire a Design

We all have times when we want to create but draw a blank as we step into the studio. Here is a simple exercise to jump-start your creativity and get you going again.

The nouns will give you ideas for a shape or motif. The verbs will give you ideas for using it. Sketch some images based on your chosen noun and verb(s). Fill several pages with ideas in your sketchbook before you settle on one to interpret in fabric. Your piece does not have to be a literal representation of the two words. The important thing is to find ideas that excite you and get you going again.

the assignment

Refer to the Introduction (page 7) for construction options.

Select a noun from the list on the left and one or more verbs from the list on the right:

NOUNS		VERBS	
Box	Boat	Distort	Bundle
Amoeba	Worm	Multiply	Turn
Fence	Piece of pie	Overlap	Interlock
Tile	Bulb	Stack	Slice
Postage stamp	Paper clip	Simplify	Divide
Stem	Doughnut	Elongate	Tilt
House	Pyramid	Fracture	Explode

the critique session

BONNY chose the noun "fence" and four different verbs: "simplify," "tilt," "multiply," and one of her own, "change direction"—one for each of the four fence post pieces. She said, "I decided to do them in the snow because I had a great snow fabric. I liked the idea of having an unexpected white foreground—we usually expect the weight of the piece (darker values) to be at the bottom of the composition." She liked the single post and the tilted ones, but found the other two unsatisfying, thinking that the fence posts should have been repeated with some subtle differences to distinguish them. She also thought the window effect was confusing, as it was unclear whether the viewer was standing inside or outside. Lorraine, however, liked the ambiguity.

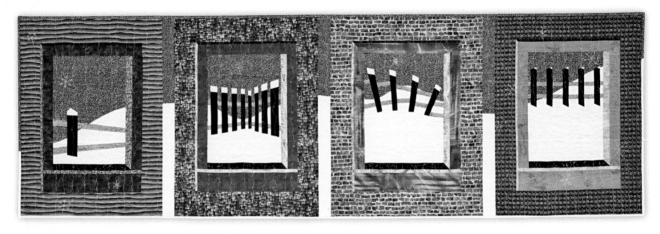

Noun: fence; verbs: simplify, change direction, tilt, multiply "Bonny found inspiration in her fabric as well as in her selected words. Inspiration is indeed all around us!" said Abbi. Ruth thought the exercise was an excellent way to create a series: pick a subject and then a series of verbs with which to manipulate the subject in each successive piece. Most of the group agreed that as separate pieces, the single post and the tilted posts were better compositions than the other two, but as a whole, the four pieces provided variety and changing scale within the repetition of the fabric, palette, and motif. Ruth thought the window frames might have distracted from the impact of the simple graphic design of the fence posts and snow, but Abbi and Amalia liked the window frame presentation and did not find it confusing. The continuous horizon line unifies the four scenes.

> ❝ To me, the fence posts are a social commentary: the one looks lonely, the seven look unified and strong, the four are free and easy, and the five are stiff and need to experience joy." – Marj

CINDY first created a visual representation of her noun, "tile," and her verb, "fracture," as separate pieces. The blue crackle glaze on a favorite ceramic pot in her home inspired her design for the verb "fracture." Then she superimposed the crackle glaze design on the tile design, inspired by the floor in a restaurant ladies' room. Duplicating the sections of the crackle glaze of her favorite pot, she cut the tile piece apart and fused it to a black fabric background, revealing slivers of black between the pieces of the fractured tile.

> The woven pattern, shattered by the fracture lines, is wonderful in its varied thickness of the cracks, the unexpected missing pieces, and the alignment of the original pattern. It makes me think of those museum pieces of Greek pottery that have been only partially reassembled." – Bonny

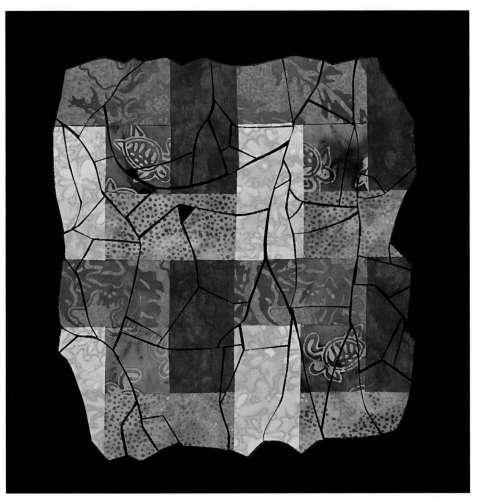

Noun: tile; verb: fracture Cindy's fractured tile piece elicited mixed responses. Abbi and Ruth liked the unpredictable combination of shapes in the tiles and the fracture lines, but Ruth, as well as Amalia, Marj, and Sharon, thought the strong shapes and vivid colors of the tiles fought with the complex, organic lines of the crackle glaze. Everyone liked the variation the missing pieces gave to the fracture lines. Everyone thought this interpretation of the two words merited more development.

RUTH "multiplied" and "overlapped" "boxes" in her exercise. She incorporated the illusion of depth to add interest to her exercise. "I worked out some designs using overlapped boxes on graph paper. Then I tried different values and colors in each polygon to create depth and secondary patterns. I chose monochromatic fabrics because they did not distract from the value placement," Ruth told us. Everyone agreed that this was a successful use of the three words, as well as a wonderful illusion of depth.

Noun: box; verbs: multiply, overlap The group all agreed that Ruth had achieved an illusion of depth with her multiplied and overlapped boxes. There was also agreement that keeping each fabric monochromatic in clearly contrasting values was the key to making the composition's strong symmetrical balance easy to read. But Bonny, while appreciative of the beautiful color, value, and balance of the piece, was disconcerted by the unpredictable dimensional effect of the relationship of the boxes, which hindered her perception of depth, and would have appreciated more consistent value placement in the boxes.

SHARON stretched the meaning of "paper clip" to include a binder clip. She added the verb "distort" and created a collage of practically living and breathing binder clips. She says she especially enjoyed the allusion to the human form, with the "legs" bending or running. It was a good exercise to stretch her abstraction skills.

Noun: paper (binder) clip; verb: distort The graphic abstraction of the clip was appreciated by most of the group. Cindy said, "This work looks like it came from a contemporary art museum." Most found the variety in the shapes of the backgrounds, the strong value contrast, and the illusion of motion achieved by the lively, changing motif very successful. Cindy liked the negative space around each motif and found that it functioned as an important element in the design—probably because of the reverse coloring in the blocks: black on brown and brown on black, and black on white and white on black. Abbi and Marj both felt, however, that there was a disjointed feeling about the composition. Both blamed the stark whiteness of the center square, which acted as a distracting element instead of an integrating one. The high-contrast, posterlike quality of the piece contributed to equally contrasting reactions to the composition among the group members.

the continuing education process

In every group critique, it becomes clear that even though you can evaluate your visual art pieces by some rather objective qualities (balance, value contrast, color, unity, and scale), there is, as they say, no accounting for taste. We all have personal experiences, subjective leanings, and differences in personality that make us prefer one thing to another and defy cut-and-dried standards in evaluating artwork. There are also quilts that seem perfect in meeting all the requirements we set for success, but that leave viewers cold.

Some designs lack that indefinable life—or spark—that lifts them out of the mundane, the predictable, the commonplace. As Lorraine frequently tells her students, learning about design elements and principles helps you train your vision and refine your subconscious decision making. But ultimately, that academic design vocabulary and the lessons you collect are best used to solve problems when they occur. A checklist (How's the value? Is there enough contrast to read the design? Is it unified, or are there too many disparate parts? Have I varied the scale, or is everything the same size?) can be extremely valuable when you have that dissatisfied feeling that something is wrong but you're not sure what it is. In the heat of the creative process, though, if things are clicking along and you are happy with your piece, keep working intuitively. All the studying you are doing in design will help develop and enrich that subterranean river of intuition.

Additional Design Exercise

For additional inspiration, collect a sketchbook full of shapes as thumbnail sketches—a shape library. Start with the simplest and most predictable shapes—such as squares, circles, or triangles—and change the shapes minutely each time you draw them. Continue until you have filled up your sketchbook, and then start another one. This time, make a line library—straight lines, curvy lines, broken lines, zigzag lines, parallel lines, and so on. You might collect other kinds of visual records—patterns, color combinations, and so on. Mark the locations of your favorites in all your collections. When you are experiencing quilter's block, open your library and find a favorite shape or line or other visual reminder. Make it the starting point for a new piece of textile art.

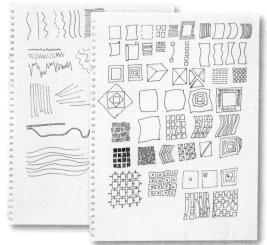

Keep shape and line libraries for inspiration.

Creativity Exercise

Collect quotes, words, phrases, poems, headlines, and so on, that inspire you. Write them out and post them in your studio or record them in your journal. When you are stuck or need a boost, reread them.

Suggested Reading

Guild, Tricia, and Elspeth Thompson. *Inspiration.* London: Quadrille Publishing, 2006.

Hire, Dianne S. *Quilters Playtime: Games with Fabrics.* Paducah, KY: American Quilter's Society, 2004.

Hire, Dianne S., ed. *Oxymorons: Absurdly Logical Quilts.* Paducah, KY: American Quilter's Society, 2001.

Weidman, Mary Lou. *Quilted Memories: Celebrations of Life.* Lafayette, CA: C&T Publishing, 2001.

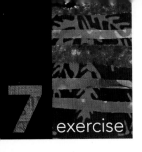
Using Images from Your Surroundings

Inspiration for your next quilt is never far away. Photographs you take on vacation, pictures in books of natural wonders or mundane subjects, scientific texts with images seen through a microscope, and even fashion magazines can be rich repositories of visual fodder. A photo, or a real scene from your kitchen window, does not have to be an image you want to render realistically in its entirety. You can use only the color palette or the visual texture of one small area of a picture or scene to give you the starting point for a successful design. The important thing is to keep your eyes open, see what you are looking at, record visual ideas in a notebook or collect them in a file folder, and refer to them when you are having a dry spell or just want to challenge yourself.

Mudflats in Death Valley
Photo by Craig Rowley

the assignment

Refer to the Introduction (page 7) for construction options.

There are three photographs, each with different visual texture and composition. Interpret one, two, or all three of the images in fabric. You may even want to create several different versions of the same photograph. Here are a few ideas:

- Isolate a small area to interpret.

- Use the photograph as an idea for a block in a repeated-block quilt.

- Rearrange the parts of the photograph in an interpretation.

- Look at the photograph once and put it away. Design your piece from what you remember seeing.

Canyon wall in the Grand Canyon
Photo by Craig Rowley

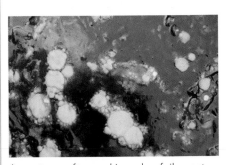

A roast pan after cooking a beef rib roast
Photo by Lorraine Torrence

the critique session

AMALIA chose to interpret the canyon wall and the mudflats. She used fusing as a technique to capture the shapes in both photos. She thought the lines in her mudflats were too straight and her canyon walls needed more value contrast to show the shadow lines more easily.

Canyon wall Amalia made her canyon wall by topstitching background pieces together and fusing narrow strips on top of them. She said she would try the exercise again with more value contrast in the fabrics so the shadow lines are easier to see. Even though the whole group liked the linear visual texture in Amalia's piece, they agreed that more contrast would have served the image better.

Mudflats The shapes in the mudflats are what captivated Amalia. Jane thought her choices of fabrics evoked softness. Everyone liked the unpredictable interpretation of the shapes in Japanese prints. The purple background fabric was dark enough to outline the shapes and the orange outlines added richness to the color scheme. The group thought the curved paths of shapes made the composition satisfying and balanced.

“ Amalia thinks her lines are too straight in the mudflats piece, but they don't seem any straighter than those in the original photo. Sometimes nature is hard to believe and we have to tweak our interpretation to make it seem real."
– Sharon

CINDY'S choices were the mudflats and the roasting pan. In the mudflats piece, the pattern of the shapes reminded her of the patterning in the hide of a giraffe. Combining the giraffe image with the mudflats pattern made her think about how much life depends on water, so she added Scrabble tiles to combine the ideas.

For her first roast pan exercise, Cindy said she wanted the grease to float so she used trapunto to make that area literally rise above the rest. She wanted the background to look shiny and wet, so she used a cut-up plastic bag over fabric and quilted circles in it. In the second, more stylized roast pan piece, she fused two fabric shapes and tried to make the background shape stand out as the focus.

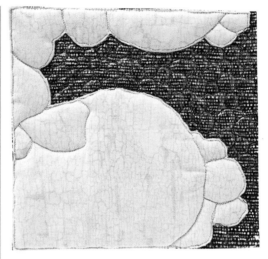

Roast pan 1 Most of the group liked the way Cindy evoked the qualities of grease with trapunto and the plastic bag in the first of her roast pan pieces, but several people thought the compositional balance had been sacrificed in Cindy's effort to capture the sense of grease. The consensus was that the piece was an interesting start for a more developed and balanced composition that she could achieve by including a dark "grease" area in the lower left corner of the piece or even expanding the area of the original photo she interpreted to find a more value-balanced and well-composed section to render in fabric.

Mudflats Everyone liked the fact that Cindy found more in the photo than the visual pattern of the mud cakes to inspire her. However, Jane, Bonny, Abbi, and Ruth all made suggestions to improve the compositional balance, such as moving the Scrabble tiles down, cropping the bottom third of the piece, or letting the dried earth design go off the edge in some places. Another idea was to arrange the Scrabble tiles in a less orderly arrangement to achieve more unity with the rest of the organic shapes.

> 66 Each of Cindy's pieces, rather than being representational, is inspired by qualities of its subject." – Jane

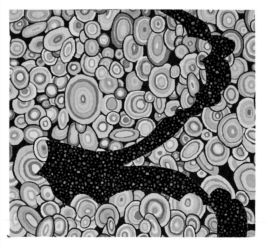

Roast pan 2 Cindy's second grease pan piece was more abstract. This time she took off with the shapes of the areas, leaving behind the interest in the grease. The dark background becomes the positive shape. Although the piece seems well balanced and meets the technical requirements for a good composition, Abbi said, "I think this a good start, but I believe the piece could use more complexity to provide more to look at and look for." The spark of interest and complexity Abbi sought could be attained by including a variety of different-sized shapes and using fabrics that have more variety in scale and value.

RUTH'S pieces were inspired by the canyon wall and roast pan photos. In the canyon walls exercise, she was drawn to the interesting lines and changes in value. Ruth used both the composition and the color palette as the basis for the roast pan piece. She was not satisfied with the balance in this piece, feeling that it was too left-heavy. She wants to remedy this in a larger piece she is planning.

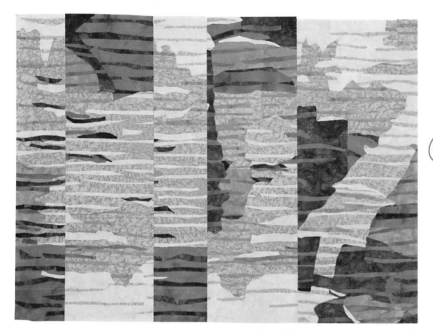

Canyon Wall Ruth fused hand-cut, irregular strips of five different values of orange and yellow to make fabric. She solved the problem of all the light being at the top and all the dark being at the bottom by slicing the piece in vertical bands of varying widths and reversing every other band. The limited, analogous color seems appropriate for the dry cliff face. There was unanimous agreement that Ruth's canyon wall interpretation was successful in every way.

> " Ruth used a specific quality from each of the photographs and built well-balanced and interesting compositions from each quality. In each piece, she has added something new that wasn't in the original photo." – Amalia

Roast pan Ruth's rendition of the roast pan was stylized to a theme of overlapping, varied-size hexagons fused on the blue background. Sharon remarked that the hexagons provided great unity, and, Jane added, variety in scale. The issue of balance was addressed by some, with suggestions for small changes such as adding a bit more blue on the lower left or removing some of the hexagons on the left. The entire group liked the composition of the piece, too.

SHARON used the canyon wall and the mudflats photos as inspiration for her pieces. She found qualities in the images to use, but did not feel compelled to depict the scenes the photos represented. In the canyon wall she saw the reverberating horizontal lines of the canyon, the heart shape, and the value changes of the wall to be the qualities she wanted to use. In the mudflats, she used only the tight but chaotic arrangement of the mud cakes in her rendition. In choosing not to depict the images themselves, she felt free to change the colors, value placement, and composition to meet the needs of her pieces.

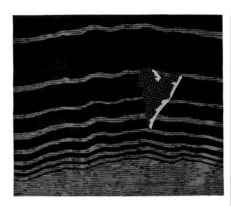

Canyon Wall Abbi noted that Sharon cut the irregular echoing lines of the green fabric in a style that was inspired by the jagged rippling of the rocks, and that using the lighter values of the green fabric at the bottom instead of at the top expressed a feeling that the reverberating lines were escaping into the universe, rather than being confined by it. Cindy thought this arrangement made it look as if the heart were creating movement or vibrations. This change in value placement created a feeling of beauty and lightness for Jane, and made it seem safe instead of rugged for Bonny. However, Ruth felt uncomfortable with it, perhaps because of the heavy blackness of the space at the top.

❝❝ Sharon used the photographs somewhat as conceptual inspiration and didn't reproduce the images exactly. Both pieces are interesting and complete as they are." – Amalia

Mudflats Although everyone appreciated the crystallographic balance in Sharon's composition, most found the connection to the photograph too remote. Bonny noted the tessellation, or nesting, of the shapes in the mudflats photo and how the individual shapes were unified to create strings of shapes. In Sharon's rendition of the photo, Bonny felt that the positive/negative relationship between the crane motif and the black background missed the unity through continuation that was present in the photo. Although not a direct depiction of the mudflats, the overall composition was successful.

the continuing education process

When you see a photograph or a real scene that inspires you to make a quilt or wallhanging, it is important to define what the important qualities or features are that you want to capture. Do you want to replicate the scene realistically? Do you want to capture a feeling the photo evokes? Do you want to abstract the piece, borrowing from it the compositional characteristics to interpret in cloth? A common risk in interpreting a scene or image is that you stay so married to the original that you are unwilling to depart from the specific characteristics of the scene or photo. In creating your original interpretation, sometimes you have to choose between staying faithful to the original or doing what your fabric piece needs to make it successful, as Sharon did in her mudflats piece. Be bold and do the latter, even if it departs from the original inspiration.

Additional Design Exercise

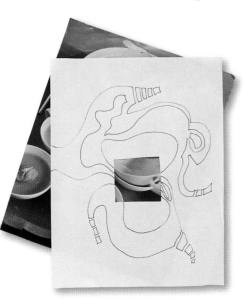

Here is an exercise that has made the rounds. It has been presented in many variations by many teachers. It is still a good one and worth including.

1. Make a window template by cutting a 2″ × 2″ hole in the middle of a piece of 8½″ × 11″ white paper.

2. Move this window template over colored pictures in magazines until you find a design, texture, color combination, or set of shapes that looks interesting to you. It may be useful to turn the magazine photograph upside down so you see the isolated photo section abstractly rather than as part of something you recognize. This will help you rely on what you are actually seeing rather than on your memory of the subject.

3. On the white paper surrounding the square hole in the paper, draw a continuation of the image in the 2″ square.

4. Simplify the design in the square and its drawn continuation.

5. Use the simplified design as the starting point for a quilt.

Creativity Exercise

Take your camera or sketchbook whenever you go for a walk. Make it a scavenger hunt. Look for something that is blue, prickly, rough, and so on. (Make up your own list.) Take photos or make sketches of everything on your walk that fits into these categories. Use the photos and sketches to germinate new ideas.

Suggested Reading

Arthus-Bertrand, Yann. *Earth from Above: 365 Days.* New York: Harry N. Abrams Publishers, 2001.

Fothergill, Alastair, Vanessa Berlowitz, and Mark Brownlow. *Planet Earth: As You've Never Seen It Before.* Berkeley, CA: University of California Press, 2008.

Frankel, Felice, and George M. Whitesides. *On the Surface of Things: Images of the Extraordinary in Science.* Cambridge, MA: Harvard University Press, 2008.

Oei, Loan, and Cecile DeKegel. *The Elements of Design: Rediscovering Colors, Textures, Forms and Shapes.* New York: Thames and Hudson, 2002.

Wolfe, Art, and Craig Childs. *The Elements: Earth, Air, Fire and Water.* Seattle, WA: Sasquatch Books, 2004.

Maintaining Unity Using Panels

Quilters often collect unique fabric panels such as screen-printed blocks, photo transfers on fabric, ethnic fabric samples, or individual antique blocks. Because the quilter usually has only one or two panels, they are seen as precious and are almost always stashed away. If the panels are used, they are most often stuck whole into a quilt or garment, surrounded with coordinating fabrics that form successive borders, or the panel is used with other fabrics chosen to carry out a conceptual theme but providing no real visual unity. Instead of seeking the cohesive visual unity of the whole piece, the preciousness of the panel is protected, thus jeopardizing its integration into the whole.

In this exercise you will practice ways to unify the whole quilt when you have a limited, unique, and often dearly held panel. You may want to practice on a panel that is part of repetitive-block or panel yardage until you are comfortable using your one-of-a-kind panel.

the assignment

Refer to the Introduction (page 7) for construction options.

Select a panel you already have, purchase a panel, or cut a panel from a commercial fabric. Make it into a piece of a different size using other fabrics that work well with it. You may practice by photo-graphing or photocopying your panel and using the picture to try out several approaches. The goal is to make a visually unified piece that uses the panel as its theme or focus fabric.

Consider visual unity—all the parts must look like they belong together. One of the most common devices for achieving unity is repetition, such as repeating a fabric, a color, a shape, a motif, or a combination of these. If you want a panel to be the visual theme or the focus fabric of your quilt, it may be a challenge to leave the panel in one piece—and thus have its fabric appear only in one place in the quilt—and still achieve visual unity. Consider your goal for the panel. Is it to integrate the piece into a larger quilt and have the panel serve as the quilt's focus, or is it to display the panel as a complete piece? Considerations are the value, the quality, and the rarity of the panel.

Here are some ideas to help you integrate panels into a quilt:

- Destroy the squareness (or rectangularity) of a panel by cutting off a corner or two and using the cut corners in other parts of the quilt. The repetition of the panel fabric is a good device for achieving unity.

- Chop up the whole thing and spread it around. Yes, even if it means cutting through images of faces!

- Try to find panels similar to the one you have, to use in the same piece. Leave one whole, per-haps, and cut the other(s) into smaller pieces.

- Try to recreate the panel (and provide unity) by duplicating the techniques, colors, design ele-ments, or other visual signatures to repeat the look of the panel.

- Sometimes the best thing to do with a special panel is simply to frame it without trying to expand it into something bigger.

the critique session

AMALIA'S panel was a batik heron piece that was a gift from her mother-in-law. She chose the coordinating fabrics by matching the colors as well as the style (more batiks) in the panel. She wanted to leave the panel as complete as possible but cut off the corners so she could repeat the fabric in other parts of the quilt. She said, "I was surprised to have achieved a unified piece without using the panel in more than one place. I reserved the corners I had cut from the original panel, but found the piece didn't improve when these corners were reapplied in other places—I think this is because of color matching." Sharon wondered if a placement other than dead center for the panel would have worked. Everyone felt that the large, undivided blocks of color provided resting places for the eyes, and that without these spaces the quilt would have been too busy.

> " Amalia successfully built a quilt around her original panel, incorporating its colors but not overwhelming it." – Abbi

The group agreed that unity and balance were achieved in the quilt, not only through color but through the circles repeating the circle in the panel, and through the fan pieced blocks, reminiscent of the birds' feathers.

Photo by Rozarii Lynch

Batik heron fabric panel

BONNY had purchased a few molas without having any idea what she would do with them. This panel exercise made Bonny think of her molas right away. "Because molas are pricey and hand stitched, I had a great deal of anxiety about cutting them," commented Bonny. In thinking about her options in using them, she spent some time with a computer drawing program, doing virtual cuts before she settled on a plan. "I attempted to give each of the mola sections a three-dimensional quality by having them appear as stacked blocks. The perspective wasn't successful, but I'm still pleased with the composition."

Mola fabric panel

> " This is the best use of molas in a larger piece I have ever seen. Bonny maintains the special character of the molas while expanding the visual field." – Ruth

Bonny left one mola whole, then cut apart three others to complete the composition. Cindy's first comment was, "That is the bravest woman I know!" She and the rest of the group liked Bonny's finished piece very much. The group as a whole disagreed with Bonny about the perspective. They thought it was subtle but effective. Everyone agreed that the piece was well unified. The addition of the cut mola pieces provided unity through repetition, and the narrow strips on the border mimicked the width of the reverse appliqué details in the piece.

JANE used an inexpensive panel from a bolt of fabric. Consequently, she felt considerably less pressure than the others in deciding what to do with it. Jane liked the color palette so she decided to create an abstract grid that kept the color placement. Jane cut the panel into 1″ squares and removed 28 groups of four squares, leaving an open grid. Then she turned the squares of the open grid on point and added some of the removed squares to create a pointed border around the open grid. After she finished, she found she had quite a pile of unused squares. She arranged them into another small composition that evoked the feeling of the original panel even though it was fractured and incomplete. "I find I often come up with unexpected and more intriguing compositions by using elements left over from the planned piece," she said.

Inexpensive fabric panel

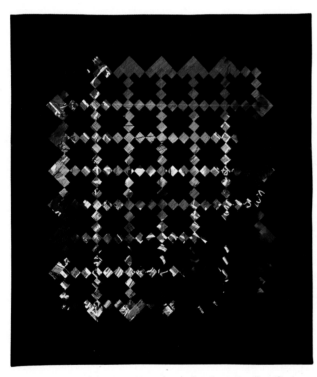

Everyone agreed that Jane's grid panel quilt was well unified and that the extra pieces she added to border it balanced the piece nicely. No one felt that giving up all reference to the original panel hurt this piece. In fact, Cindy thought Jane had won the gold when she destroyed the ugly panel and replaced it with a praiseworthy quilt.

Abbi felt that this second panel quilt made with Jane's leftovers was the real showstopper. As a subtle reference to the poster quality of the original panel, the small quilt became, for Bonny, a much more interesting composition, with the visual weight of the strong purple on the right balancing the bright yellow and orange of the bridge on the left.

❝❝ In the grid piece, I love the way some of the darker areas seem to melt into the background. It keeps the grid from being static." – Marj

the continuing education process

Unity is important in any work of art, but as visual artists we must understand the difference between **visual** and **conceptual** unity. **Conceptual unity** means cohesiveness of the idea or the theme, even if the style or the manner in which it is interpreted in different parts is different. **Visual unity** has to do with **how** the concepts or ideas are presented. Visual unity is achieved when the **presentation** of the ideas is executed in a similar way.

Our exercise on unity was made more challenging because of the additional requirement of using a panel in the quilt. Because repetition is the most common device for achieving unity, the natural way to accomplish unity in the panel exercise is to repeat the panel, or parts of it. This means reproducing the panel, or elements from it, or cutting it up. That is difficult for most people to do. The three students whose panel exercises are in this chapter were able to unify their quilts very well—all in different ways. But unity is a requirement for any quilt you make, whether you use a panel or not. When looking at any quilt, ask yourself the following questions:

- Do the parts of my quilt look like they belong together, or are the parts too different?

- What device(s) have I used to unify my quilt? Repetition? Proximity? Continuation? (See Additional Design Exercise, below.)

- Have I confused conceptual unity (cohesiveness of the idea or subject matter) with visual unity (consistency of the presentation of the elements in the interpretation of the idea)?

Additional Design Exercise

Two other methods for achieving unity are **proximity** and **continuation**. Sometimes, simply moving elements in a visual field closer together will make the piece look more visually unified. This is **unity through proximity**. When they are closer together, the parts have more to do with each other than when they are separated. Arranging the elements in a line of some kind (straight, zigzagged, curved, spiraled) so they are more related is another way to achieve visual unity. This is **unity through continuation**.

The following is a simple exercise to try out these concepts:

1. Prepare 8–10 pieces of fabric for fusing. Cut 1 piece of fabric into 3 pieces and stack the 3 pieces right side up. From the stack, cut 2 or 3 different shapes, yielding 3 identical pieces of each shape from the same fabric. Repeat this step with each piece of fabric. As you cut each shape, separate the pieces into 3 identical piles.

2. Cut 3 identical background pieces from 1 fabric. On 1 background, randomly arrange the fusible-backed shapes from 1 pile so the shapes are spread out all over the surface, with about equal spacing between the shapes—like an explosion on the surface. Fuse the final design in place.

3. On the second background, randomly arrange the second pile of shapes (identical to the pile you arranged on the first background) into one or more clusters so your eyes have one or more focal points to connect as they scan the design. Fuse the final design in place.

4. On the third background, align the third pile of shapes in some kind of continuous line. Fuse the final design in place.

Random arrangement This arrangement does not look unified because the eye doesn't know where to focus. It doesn't make sense.

Linear arrangement Lining up the shapes in this curvy line also unifies this piece. The diverse shapes are now related because they are all part of the same linear shape.

Creativity Exercise

Look for unity in all that you see. Look at advertisements, quilts, paintings, photos, and gardens. Ask yourself if what you see is well unified. If so, what makes it so? If not, what would you do to make it more unified?

Suggested Reading

Dantzic, Cynthia Maris. *Design Dimensions: An Introduction to the Visual Surface*. Englewood Cliffs, NJ: Prentice Hall, 1990.

Lauer, David, and Stephen Pentak. *Design Basics*. 6th ed. Belmont, CA: Thompson Wadsworth, 2005.

Torrence, Lorraine. *Design Essentials: The Quilter's Guide*. Seattle, WA: Lorraine Torrence Designs, 2008.

Wong, Wucius. *Principles of Form and Design*. New York: Van Nostrand Reinhold, 1993.

Clustered arrangement When the same shapes are moved closer together to form three clusters, the eye has a path to follow, and the interim spaces help define the focal points. Even though the shapes are abstract, the viewer understands what's happening here.

Designing Borders and Quilting

Borders and quilting, for many quilters, are two common obstacles to completing a successful quilt. At either or both of these steps in the process you may stop and agonize about what to do next. You know the quilt needs to reflect a unified and well-developed whole, rather than the borders and quilting appearing to be disconnected afterthoughts.

Your quilt may not need a border. In fact, you may not want even the additional line of a binding, choosing instead to face the quilt's edge. Make these judgments visually. Audition several options on your design wall before you settle on a border, or absence of one, that gives your quilt just the finale it needs. There may be more than one option that pleases you. In fact, there is usually more than one right way to do everything.

Indecision about how to quilt is a common dilemma. Experience and experimentation are the best hedges against this common problem. Again, there are probably several good solutions to the quilting challenge.

In this exercise, you will do some experimenting that will add to your experience of finding good solutions for both borders and quilting. You can decide which combinations you like best when you are finished; keep them all as ideas for later use.

the assignment

1. Make 3 or 4 (or more) identical small quilts, about 14″–16″ square.

2. Design and add a different border to each of your quilts. Make sure each of the borders complements and enhances the quilt.

3. Layer, baste, and machine or hand quilt each of the small quilts in a different way. Vary not only the stitching designs but the thread colors and types as well.

4. Bind, face, or otherwise finish the edges, as appropriate for each small quilt.

ABBI said she is one of those quilters who follows the path of least resistance when it comes to borders. For her, adding cornerstones to a border constitutes dressing it up. The border part of the assignment was a challenge for her, but she felt her quilting was more successful because she has had more practice. Yes, practice really does make a difference.

Abbi chose to add a simple, traditional three-strip border of different widths using the Asian floral print separated by a 1/4" strip of the dark green of the center square. Ruth liked the liveliness of the thin line. (Remember the scale lesson on page 32?) Metallic gold thread in floral, leaf, and wavy-line quilting designs accents the organic nature of the focus fabric.

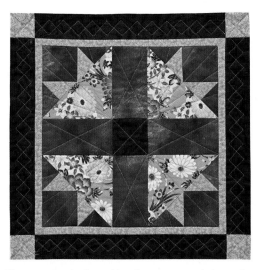

This very simple, formal border was a good choice for Abbi's quilt, as was the yellow-gold cotton thread quilting in a geometric and symmetrical pattern that everyone thought enhanced the block. Sometimes the simplest choices are what a quilt really needs.

This asymmetrical border on a very symmetrical block was the least favorite of everyone in the group. Most thought the border detracted from the block rather than enhancing it. The group saw Abbi's overall meandering flowering-vine quilting as unrelated to the quilt and would have preferred something that had more unifying appeal.

Most of the group liked the movement provided by the elongated white triangles surrounding this block. Some thought the curving quilting lines enhanced that movement, and others felt it was not as compatible with the geometry of the block as straight-line quilting would have been.

CINDY designed this interesting four-unit positive/negative block with a lighter square woven through the four red squares. She says she has never been a quilter who thinks about borders. Just a single piece of fabric to frame the top has always been her game plan, so this assignment was a challenge.

Cindy's block was placed on point in this quilt. When she added bordered triangles made of one of the fabrics in the block, it created a floating block that extends into the border. Everyone agreed that of all Cindy's quilts, this quilt's border was the most integrated with the block design. Cindy quilted in the ditch and highlighted some of the strips forming the overlapping squares. The group said that what she had done sufficiently accentuated those areas but that more needed to be done to balance the density of the quilting overall.

Everyone thought that this wide, single-fabric border was not as successful as the border on the first quilt because the width was too great compared to the width of the pieced inner boxes. Others thought that the value of the border drowned the quilt, and that the introduction of this new fabric failed to unify the quilt. Sharon loved the border fabric so much that she focused more on the dominant border and didn't pay much attention to the quilt. Cindy repeated the curlicues of the border fabric as quilting in contrasting thread in much of the interior of the piece, enabling the quilting to be visually unified with other elements in this design.

66 Cindy's interesting block creates optical illusions and a lot of movement." – Jane

In Cindy's third quilt, the strong mustard-yellow border with its narrow red lines added zing, interest, and a change of scale for some of the group, while others thought it was unrelated to the interior. The maze quilting pattern seemed the most interesting and most related to the quilt.

JANE used a simple nine-patch with black triangles edging the red squares for her block. The mottled fabrics she used provide added texture, but the borders are really what give the blocks their interesting designs.

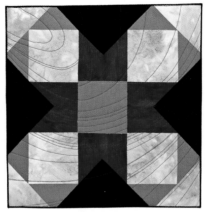

A dark border provides a window effect, as if the viewer is looking from the inside to a light sky outside. The red rectangle and green triangle at the center of each side extend the design of the interior to integrate and unify the quilt. Ruth thought the curving parallel lines of the quilting added a flow that didn't conflict with the straight-edged design.

Jane's border in this example becomes such an extension of the block that it functions less like a border and more like an enlargement of the block design. Ruth remarked that Jane's swirling quilting lines added a feeling of air and wind currents that works with the light gray mottled fabric.

Sharon felt that the thin black strips introducing the border of this piece mimicked stained glass, and she preferred the other, more elegant renditions. Bonny thought the black strips were unlike any other shape in the interior of the block and therefore were not a unifying feature, but rather a bit out of place. Others found this to be another interesting variation in the collection. Jane's angular parallel-line quilting maintained the angled geometry of the pieced design, while its less predictable pattern added interest to the symmetry of the piecing.

 Jane took a unique approach to this exercise by challenging the concept of separate borders. In each piece she created an outer row that is so at one with the center that I hesitate to call it a border."
– Abbi

The simple addition of more light gray mottled fabric creates ghostlike edges and corners on the original block that are barely visible. Centered black triangles on each side extend the block design to the edges. Sharon thought the variation in the space between the quilting lines added interest and softened some of the formality of the block.

Another interesting addition to the original block produces a black batlike shape that gives life and the illusion of motion to this collection of otherwise geometric shapes. The quilting lines enhance that illusion of motion.

MARJ used an uneven eight-pointed star design with nine-patch corners for her block. Each block varies slightly because of the shapes and fabrics chosen for the star points. Unusual fabrics and the wacky star points give the block a whimsical rather than a formal feeling.

The hot pink border on Marj's first block repeats the pink within the block and keeps it unified. Sharon and Ruth both commented on the successful effect created by the extension of the small star points into the borders at the corners. The sharing of the small white corner squares by the nine-patches of the interior block and the border's corner stars inextricably links the border to the block. Marj outline quilted the shapes in white thread, letting the thread show. She echo quilted in the white areas and left the colored area unquilted. This method of quilting did not compete with the piecing and functioned to accentuate the shapes, sometimes in an unexpected way, especially when the white stitched star points continued into the border to complete those shapes.

The simple three-strip border in varying widths calms the busy block with the use of simplicity and soothing color. Sharon liked the way the quilting lines flowed from the piecing lines. Bonny found the quilting in all the blocks to be utilitarian without adding anything to the compositions.

Nearly everyone in the group thought this strong border over-powered the lively, playful block, even though the squares in the border repeated the nine-patch squares in the block. Outlining the nine-patch and continuing the straight line from one corner nine-patch to another, crossing a section of star points, seemed less unified than Marj's quilting designs in other blocks.

This border received mixed reviews. Abbi liked the two kinds of border treatment but thought the wider pink line on the right should have extended to the top edge. Jane thought the border was too asymmetrical for this block. Bonny felt that the asymmetry was in keeping with the wackiness of the block but that the two border fabrics did not contrast enough to show the design. Marj kept the same tone of wackiness in her quilting, and she took off in unpredictable directions with her straight-line white-thread quilting in the interior of the block. Most thought the quilting didn't really enhance the piecing, though.

66 In each case, Marj used great fabric choices and quilting to tie the border to the interior of the quilt."
– Abbi

the continuing education process

A good way to audition borders for a quilt is to photograph the quilt and make several paper picture frames for the photo. You can sketch different border ideas on each frame and leave one frame blank, representing a faced edge. Audition each border option with the quilt photo. Use colored marking pens or pencils to simulate the colors and values in the proposed border fabrics. Seeing is really the best way to make a decision in a visual medium. As Lorraine has said to her students for many years, **make visual decisions visually!**

Audition different border ideas on paper frames around photos of the quilt.

Additional Design Exercise

In Using Words to Inspire a Design (starting on page 53), your additional exercise was to create a line library and a shape library. Now try a quilting design library. Fill a sketchbook with thumbnail sketches of line patterns that could be used to quilt all or part of a quilt. You might divide your quilting pattern library into categories such as the following:

- Straight lines
- Curvy lines
- Grid patterns
- Geometric shapes
- Organic shapes
- Combination patterns (a mixture of two or more categories)

Although each quilt will require an individualized quilting solution, your library of quilting designs will be a good resource for ideas.

Creativity Exercise

When designing the borders, quilting patterns, or other finishing elements, do a mental check to see if you have built "fences" around your ability to be creative. Sometimes we can get stuck in what we know and have always done, rather than focusing on what we creatively dream. Look at your work and the work of others. Make a list of five ways to finish your quilt, and try what you have never tried before. Make it a personal goal to try these techniques. Explore different borders as well as finishing options. Experimenting with different techniques is vital to developing new ideas.

Suggested Reading

Collins, Sally. *Borders, Bindings and Edges: The Art of Finishing Your Quilt.* Lafayette, CA: C&T Publishing, 2004.

Crust, Melody, and Heather Waldron Tewell. *A Fine Line: Techniques and Inspirations for Creating the Quilting Design.* Chicago: Quilt Digest Press, 2002.

Florence, Judy. *Creative Designs for Hand and Machine Quilting.* Saddlebrook, NJ: EZ International, 1996.

Noble, Maurine. *Machine Quilting Made Easy.* Woodinville, WA: That Patchwork Place, 1994.

Sandbach, Kathy. *Show Me How to Plan My Quilting.* Lafayette, CA: C&T Publishing, 2007.

Torrence, Lorraine. *Shifting Perspectives.* Lafayette, CA: C&T Publishing, 2006.

Designing and Working with Pattern

Fabric is an addiction for most of us who quilt. We buy it, we collect it, some of us are afraid to cut into it, and all of us love to arrange it. For most of us, our favorite thing to do with it is to combine it with other fabrics to make wonderful groups stacked neatly in a pile, ready for the day when we have time to embark on a special project. The thing most of us **don't** do with fabric, however, is design it. We like a new line when it is introduced in our local quilt shop, but we seldom give any thought to what makes a successful line of fabrics.

In this exercise you will have the chance to design a line of fabrics and then use your fabrics to make a small quilt. Doing this will give you a new appreciation for a beautiful line of fabrics, and perhaps introduce you to the world of surface design.

the assignment

Refer to the Introduction (page 7) for construction options.

Design three coordinating pieces of fabric. You may use any method you like to create the fabric: piecing, painting, printing, stamping, stenciling, resist dying techniques, computer graphics, fusing, or any other technique that suits your fancy. Plan your three pieces so they will coordinate in color, scale, and motif.

1. Design and create your fabrics using any technique. Make enough of each fabric so you will have a sample left over when your quilt is finished.

- Design a stripe.

- Design a stylized pattern using a natural form (fish, leaf, tree, flower, fruit, vegetable, and so on), a number, a letter, or a geometric shape. Make the design either random or regular.

- Design an overall background pattern using lines, shapes, or images of some kind. Make the pattern small and either random or regular. Superimpose another shape on the background fabric in a regular pattern.

2. Combine your 3 fabrics in a small quilt. You may add other fabrics if you like.

the critique session

JANE designed and made not three but over ten different fabrics to use in her quilt. She chose a leaf/tree theme, and stamped and printed the motifs on commercial solid-color cottons. She made stripes by cutting and fusing together strips of the solid fabrics in various widths. Ultimately, she did not use the stripes in her quilt. Jane said it became immediately clear how difficult a job the fabric designer has in coming up with designs that are interesting in themselves but at the same time valuable for cutting up and combining in a quilt design.

Jane's completed quilt block

Large printed leaf design

Dark tree stamps with dotted background

Dark tree stamps with plain background

Random printed leaf design, light on dark

Mottled design with dark tree stamps

Random printed leaf design, dark on light

Overlapping tree stamps

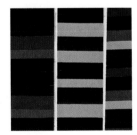

Pieced stripes

Striped variations

Everyone agreed that Jane had outdone herself in making beautiful fabrics printed with acrylic paint from leaves in her garden, a tree stamp, and the end of a paint-brush, achieving a good variety of scale. Most agreed with Jane's decision not to use the striped fabric from the collection in her quilt.

> " Jane's fabric is elegant, unified, and usable. It is important that she didn't feel she had to use all the fabric prints she made." – Cindy

Everyone admired Jane's quilt. Abbi summed it up by saying that Jane's quilt was very appealing because of the visual textures in the stamped fabric. Her repeated use of the alternating blocks creates unity while the orientation of the blocks adds variety.

MARJ decided to use her fabric ideas to make complete quilt blocks instead of just fabric. The two blocks incorporate a plaid (a combination of two stripes) and a flower block behind a picket fence. Marj slashed through the flower block and spread its pieces apart to reveal narrow strips of yellow background behind the pieces.

Flower focus-fabric block

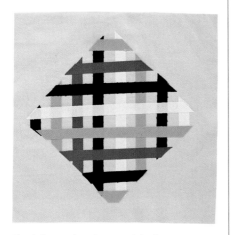

Plaid design for alternate block

The picket fence has slats the same width as the stripes in the plaid, which some called unifying and others called less interesting because it doesn't contain as much variety. Everyone liked the difference between the focus-fabric flower block, with its dark and dominant background, and the supporting role played by the plaid in the alternate block.

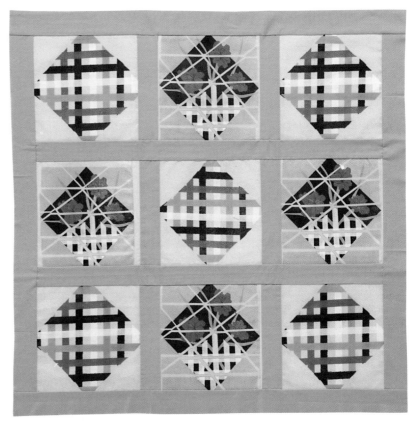

Jane astutely commented that placing the flowers behind the picket fence could have represented the end of the fabric design process, and cutting through them to create the yellow slashes might have been left for the quiltmaking process. Creating completed blocks for the fabric did not leave many options for using the fabric in a quilt. But the group did think the finished quilt was unusual, balanced, and successful with its unique color scheme and well-chosen lime green sashing.

66 She took a really novel pattern design technique and made something traditional-looking with unit blocks that alternate."
— Amalia

SHARON has been collecting tracings of the hands of family members for several years and decided to use them to make this quilt featuring her own bridge game theme fabrics. For the bridge table covering, Sharon started with her own hand-dyed fabric and stamped on it using textile paint on the ends of bamboo skewers and chopsticks. The cards were hand painted on fabric and then cut into card shapes. Sharon used commercial stamps to decorate some of the hand-dyed fabric for the border. She pieced the striped border using her hand-stamped border fabric, her hand-dyed fabrics, and strips of brown commercially made fabric that reminded her of Bridge Mix candy. The fabric used for the hands was a commercial fabric.

Hand-painted playing cards

Commercial stamps decorate the border fabrics.

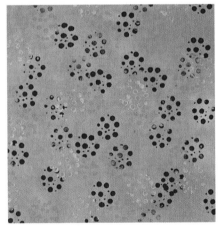

Bundles of bamboo skewers and chopsticks were used to stamp interesting motifs.

The three fabrics Sharon made incorporated three scales in different surface design techniques. Everyone agreed that the combination worked well together.

Sharon's story of the bridge games that were a regular part of her family history made an interesting context for using her unique handmade fabrics. The members of the group all felt that the quilt was successful in balance, color, and unity. Bonny and Amalia thought darker values in the interior of the quilt would have created more balance. Bonny suggested that a small line of the dark brown found in the border could be used somewhere in the cards—possibly a faint shadow behind the cards or a line in the border of the cards—which would bring darker values into the interior of the quilt and help the cards stand out on the background of the card table. Lorraine especially liked that the one green square on the tabletop was balanced by the two green borders on the opposite side.
Photo by Mark Frey

66 Sharon first decided on the elements of the quilt and then designed the fabric, allowing her to produce the correct scales, shapes, and colors for the final quilt. This is the best reason for designing your own fabric."
– Ruth

the continuing education process

When you choose fabrics at the store for a quilt, you consciously select fabrics that vary in scale, value, and color, but still coordinate. Designing fabrics to use in a quilt requires the same attention to variety within a coordinating range. Most commercial fabric lines are produced in a range of designs, but also in several colorways. Usually there is some crossover between the colorways. For example, you can often use a design from one colorway with pieces in a different scale from another colorway. Frequently, the addition of other fabrics from different lines or even manufacturers is necessary if you want to keep your fabric combination from looking predictable or even uninteresting. When everything matches too perfectly in color, there is less vibrancy and richness. Don't be afraid to expand your fabric choices.

Additional Design Exercise

In this chapter's assignment, you may have started your fabric design process by choosing the method of surface design first and then designing different pieces that fell within the capabilities of your technique. Expand your experimentation by trying the following surface design exercise:

1. Choose a multicolored commercial fabric that you like.

2. Ask yourself what you would be inclined to coordinate with it—for example, colors, patterns, designs, stripes, motifs, and so on. In a sketchbook, record your ideas.

3. Based on the designs you recorded in your sketchbook, select 1 or 2 appropriate forms of surface design and produce the coordinating fabric that will work well with the commercial fabric.

4. Now, take the commercial fabric out of the mix. Using your chosen form (or forms) of surface design, create a fabric to replace the commercial fabric that inspired you. Try not to duplicate the fabric, but design something new that will go with the coordinates you designed in Step 3.

5. Use the fabrics you created in a quilt. Add additional fabrics as needed.

Creativity Exercise

Look at your designs, exercises, and finished pieces. Analyze them, and write a critique in another person's voice (that of your teacher or someone whose work you admire). Try to come up with five objective observations (refer back to The Critique Process, starting on page 11). If there is a consistent observation in your comments, perhaps you have discovered something you want to keep doing, or something that you want to change in your work.

Suggested Reading

Dunnewold, Jane. *Complex Cloth: A Comprehensive Guide to Surface Design*. Bothell, WA: Fiber Studio Press, 1996.

Gillman, Rayna. *Create Your Own Hand-Printed Cloth: Stamp, Screen & Stencil with Everyday Objects*. Lafayette, CA: C&T Publishing, 2008.

Jerstorp, Karin, and Eva Kohlmark. *The Textile Design Book*. New York: Lark Books, 1988.

Kahn, Sherril. *Creating with Paint: New Ways, New Materials*. Woodinville, WA: Martingale and Co., 2001.

Koolish, Lynn. *Fast, Fun & Easy Fabric Dyeing: Create Colorful Fabric for Quilts, Crafts & Wearables*. Lafayette, CA: C&T Publishing, 2008.

Laury, Jean Ray. *Imagery on Fabric: A Complete Surface Design Handbook*. Lafayette, CA: C&T Publishing, 1997.

Lawler, Mickey. *Skydyes: A Visual Guide to Fabric Painting*. Lafayette, CA: C&T Publishing, 1999.

Messent, Jan. *Designing with Pattern*. London: Crochet Design, 1992.

Noble, Elin. *Dyes and Paints*. East Freetown, MA: Elin Noble, 2003.

working
in a **series**

The third part of the design course has a different structure. Instead of doing exercises, you move on to self-guided work. You have had some practice exploring design elements and principles, and you have spent some time looking at sources and inspiration. Now you are ready to use the design lessons you've explored to create finished work. Instead of dabbling in several styles, you will concentrate on series work.

Getting Started

What Is Series Work?

Series work is several, or many, pieces that all explore the same theme or visual direction. The concept, motif, technical approach, or other consistent thread should be maintained. Each piece in the group should look like it is part of a continuum, and all the pieces should look like they belong together. There should be an evolution as your series progresses. Each quilt should generate the next. As you are working on your first quilt, you may think of something to add to the second quilt that will improve or enhance it. You may think about how a piece is successful in most ways but lacks energy (or color richness, or visual texture, or something else) and that you'd like to try to remedy the problem when you make the next one. Frequently, the first quilts in a series are small and manageable, but as you get further along in the series, the quilts grow in size, complexity, and, often, technical challenges.

Where to Start

Some students who reach the third year of design study have a clear-cut idea of what they want to do in their series. They have an idea or theme they want to use, they know which technique they want to use, and they have a vision of how the first quilt might look.

Those who struggle to get started with a series usually have one of two problems: they are drawing a complete blank (no ideas), or their heads are swimming with a plethora of ideas and they are trying to figure out ways to use all of them.

If you are one without a clear idea, I usually suggest you choose an exercise from the first or second section of this course. Plan how you would extend the exercise into a three- or four-quilt series that goes beyond the original exercise and develop it in a certain direction.

If you have many ideas and feel like combining them or jumping around with them, try this:

1. Create 3 columns on a piece of paper.

2. In the first column, list all the ideas you have for content, a concept, or a theme.

3. In the second column, list all the techniques you are thinking you'd like to use in your series.

4. In the third column, list any visual goals you have for the work. For instance, you might want to explore asymmetrical balance in all your pieces, or you might want to work in as close a value range as you can while providing just enough contrast for viewers to "read" the piece.

As much as you'd like to mix all these together in your series, select only one entry from each column. Be patient about the other things you are eager to do. You can start another series after you've explored one idea, in one technique, with one visual goal. The purpose of a series, after all, is to do something long enough to get good at it and long enough to develop your idea until it is no longer going anywhere.

How Long to Work On a Series

Try to pursue your series concept until you have made at least three or four quilts. If you are not happy with the first piece in your series, don't abandon the series. Keep working on it until you solve the problems you identified in the first piece. When you have explored everything you can in your concept, and when your quilts no longer improve or take the concept to new places, chances are you'll be bored and want to start a new series. Many of the students who stay in Lorraine's Design III classes from year to year choose a different series each year. Others spend two or three years on the same series. Marj has been working on the same series since her first Design III class eight years ago. Many of the most famous art quilters have worked on one series for over fifteen years.

Remember: quantity generates quality!

Student Series Work

Abbi

Photo by Jane Koura

I am very drawn to geometric shapes. The series shown here is based on squares and rectangles, hence the name Boxes. The idea came to me when I heard a story of a garage so full of stored boxes that stacks of them had started to fall over. *Boxes II* uses the same shapes as *Boxes I* but moves from the static state of the first piece to a piece that implies action. *Boxes III* is larger and brighter but still shows motion; this factory is more attractive than the one in *Boxes II*, but it is very robotic—the antithesis of the creativity we experience in our work with fibers. I will continue with the Boxes series to make more statements about the materialistic world.

Boxes I

Boxes II

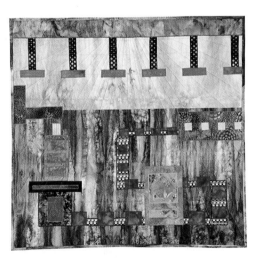

Boxes III

Boxes I, Abbi Barden, 18¼″ × 19¼″, 2007. This quilt is a statement about having too much stuff.

Boxes II, Abbi Barden, 23½″ × 14½″, 2007. This quilt reflects how the manufacturing of excess belongings dirties our environment

Boxes III, Abbi Barden, 24½″ × 23½″, 2008. This quilt speaks to the increasing sterility of a manufacturing process in which people are no longer involved in a hands-on way in the production of material goods.

Amalia

Photo by Jane Koura

note

Amalia's designs for this series have been published as a quilt pattern called Sunspots by Lorraine Torrence Designs Quilt Pattern Series and is available at www. lorrainetorrence.com.

The first quilt in this series, with overlapping circles, had a very complicated piecing order and wasn't fun to make. I liked the design and kept trying to design the pattern so it would look the same but be less stressful to make. Vertical panels that interrupt the circles make piecing much simpler. In the first pieces I challenged myself to use as little value variation as possible while still providing some interest and separation between sections. Later, I experimented with appliquéd circles and yin-yang symbols in the centers of the large circles. Next, I tried fabric from other countries, seeing how large a scale of print I could use and still have the different sections look distinct.

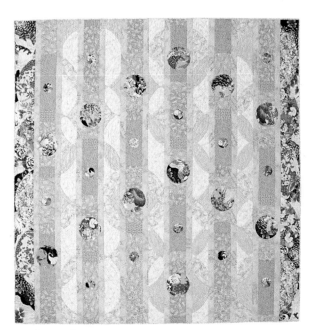

Circle Panel #4

Circle Panel #5

Circle Panel #7

Circle Panel #4, Amalia Magaret, 88″ × 94″, 2005. This is a close-value piece using Japanese-style fabrics.

Circle Panel #5, Amalia Magaret, 47½″ × 60½″, 2005. This is a later piece using African fabrics.

Circle Panel #7, Amalia Magaret, 48″ × 61″, 2008. Using Indonesian batik, the same fabric is used in all parts of each circle to make the circle look whole, de-emphasizing the panels.

Bonny

Photo by Jane Koura

I aspire to show the viewer a place that he or she might not have seen before. Because of my years as a scientist and educator, inspiration often comes from the cellular or molecular world. The ideas for the Button series come from micrographs of cells. In each piece, the buttons or beads in these quilts represent the DNA of cells, identical in cells from the same individual but different in cells from different individuals. From the mundane (onion) to the grotesque (tumors), microscopy can reveal underlying beauty. I see this series expanding to include *Gut Feelings*, *In a Heartbeat*, and *Skin Deep*. I can't wait to see where the next micrographs take me.

A Drop in the Bucket

Gene Pool

Bad News

A Drop in the Bucket, Bonny Brewer, 31″ × 40½″, 2005. This quilt shows the cells of an onion root in neat rows creating a tessellated plane.

Gene Pool, Bonny Brewer, 36″ × 24″, 2005. In this quilt, the cells became the focal point to create an overall pattern.

Bad News, Bonny Brewer, 37″ × 51½″, 2008. This quilt illustrates how cells can sometimes go crazy, causing uncontrolled cell division, as in breast cancer.

Cindy

Photo by Jane Koura

My series started after taking a class with fiber artist Rosalie Dace. I fell in love with the technique and started making small wall quilts with skinny lines and faced edges. All the quilt titles have the word "line" in them. I have finished seven pieces in the series and intend to continue with it. I have been trying for two years to settle on a series that excites me, and I'm finally getting the feel for what I'm doing. I never wanted to do series work. I thought doing the same thing over and over would be boring, but now I have found that I'm really more creative this way—exploring new ways to employ this technique.

Line Dance

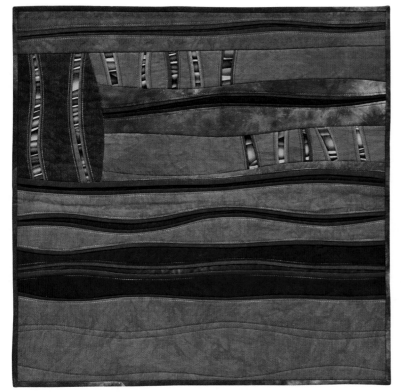

Line of Sight

Fault Line

Line Dance, Cindy Hayes, 15″ × 21½″, 2006. This quilt was the first in the series and was made in Rosalie Dace's class. I named the quilt **Line Dance** in tribute to the class by the same name.

Line of Sight, Cindy Hayes, 21¾″ × 21″, 2006. In the second quilt in the series, the emphasis is on more open space, thus the name **Line of Sight**.

Fault Line, Cindy Hayes, 15¾″ × 21½″, 2007. Growing up in California made me constantly aware of earthquakes and fault lines. The pillars at the bottom remind me of the cracks in asphalt

Jane

Photo by Jane Koura

I've sketched these shapes for a long time. After participating in a class on using fusible web, I realized that I could put my doodles into fabric.

In each piece, I bordered the top and bottom with black bands of different widths. I think that helps to emphasize the vertical lines of each element. I floated parts and pieces into these borders and used predominately hand-dyed fabrics with various decorative and satin stitches. I'm pleased with the series—the colors, the vibrancy, and the oddity of the shapes thrill me.

Stems and Leaves

Stems and Leaves with Green

Stems and Leaves with Blue

Stems and Leaves, Jane Koura, 36″ × 24″, 2005. To showcase the stems and leaves, I created flowers with interesting foliage for this first quilt in the series.

Stems and Leaves with Green, Jane Koura, 39″ × 33″, 2005. This piece uses very large, prominent green bulbs.

Stems and Leaves with Blue, Jane Koura, 37″ × 30″, 2005. I liked the lined-up look but wanted to go a little further with the idea, so this piece includes the bulbs without any flowers. I cut this piece apart into a triptych to improve the composition.

Marj

Photo by Jane Koura

The inspiration for my Tile Quilt series was the wall tiles in the River Walk retail area in San Antonio, Texas. My first piece had many of the same design elements as the wall tiles. I started with small, symmetrical designs. As I began drawing and planning my designs on paper, the quilts started to become asymmetrical, making them more pleasing—but also more challenging—to construct. I enjoy using many different types and textures of cotton fabrics. I like the unexpected combination of unusual fabrics with traditional shapes. I have struggled technically with the precision this approach requires, but during the eight years I have been working on this series my piecing has become more exact with the use of paper piecing. Some of the quilts have taken a year to complete.

Tile Quilt #5

Tile Quilt #9

Tile Quilt #10

Tile Quilt #5, Marjorie Brost, 40½″ × 40½″, 2005. This early piece features a symmetrical medallion.

Tile Quilt #9, Marjorie Brost, 43″ × 33½″, 2007. Asymmetry was the next step in my series.

Tile Quilt #10, Marjorie Brost, 54″ × 77″, 2008. This is the first experiment with very light-value background tile blocks.

Ruth

Photo by Jane Koura

Observing nature opens a vast array of creative possibilities to me, producing sensations I want to interpret in fabric.

A favorite technique is piecing and chopping—it doesn't allow for complete control and I enjoy the serendipity of the unusual color and shape combinations that result. I create some regularity with squares, which lets me move whole blocks of color and value around to produce a complete picture based on my original perceptions. These quilts were designed as couch quilts, with the intention of viewing them on a horizontal plane with hills and valleys affecting what part of the quilt would be most visible at any one time. The exploration of color combinations has given me the courage to put almost any group of colors together, making them work based on value and intensity.

Woodland Perceptions I

Woodland Perceptions II

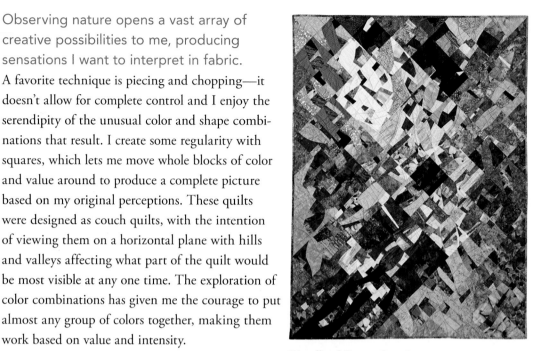

Woodland Perceptions III

Woodland Perceptions I, Ruth Vincent, 42¾″ × 57″, 2005. Trees in the landscape with lush green branches and flamboyant blooms inspired this piece.

Woodland Perceptions II, Ruth Vincent, 43½″ × 63¾″, 2006. This quilt began from gnarled, dried trunks against a blue sky.

Woodland Perceptions III, Ruth Vincent, 42″ × 63½″, 2006. Changing leaves overhanging a fast-flowing stream were the inspiration for this third quilt in the series.

Sharon

Photo by Jane Koura

These three quilts were created for the YWCA Angeline's Center for Homeless Women, which I have long supported. The unifying theme is the image of hands in motion, which suggests to me the ability to change one's world for the good. Each piece honors a different aspect of the shelter. To make the hands compelling, we photographed my arms in action in directed light and used a computer program to posterize the images, simplifying them into two or three values.

Angeline's Promise
Photo by Craig Rowley

Alice's Garden
Photo by Craig Rowley

Rita's Vision
Photo by Craig Rowley

Angeline's Promise, Sharon Rowley, 43″ × 58″, 2003. **Angeline's Promise**, with hands climbing over a brick wall, honors the clients and their hopes.

Alice's Garden, Sharon Rowley, 39″ × 46″, 2003. **Alice's Garden**, with hands watering a healthy garden, honors the fundraisers.

Rita's Vision, Sharon Rowley, 46″ × 52″, 2003. **Rita's Vision**, with hands catching a star, captures the vision of the staff.

Summing Up

Finally, we offer you suggestions for starting your own critique group so you can practice talking about your and others' work and expanding your design skills in a supportive and comfortable environment. Our eight students have the last words with their thoughts on creating.

Starting Your Own Critique Group

A group of quilting friends dedicated to critiquing each other's work, sharing ideas, and offering support for each other can make a dramatic difference in the quality and quantity of your work. It can boost your confidence and expose you to new ways of thinking about your work. If you are convinced of the benefits, the next task is to find a group of equally convinced quilters and plan your first meeting.

Here are a few things to consider:

- A small number is better than no one, but a group of at least six or eight starts to provide diversity of opinion and a wider range of work to look at.

- Usually the most convenient meeting places are the members' homes. If your group reaches numbers too great to fit comfortably in someone's living room or recreation room, consider meeting in a public library meeting room, a community center, or your local quilt shop's classroom. If you have to pay for meeting space, it may make your group take the meeting more seriously.

- Select a discussion leader. It is a good idea to take turns sharing this responsibility. Being the discussion leader provides good practice in focusing your own critical thinking. Agree on a meeting and critique format.

- Challenge each other with exercises you write yourselves or find in books.

- Think about mounting a show at some point when your work seems exhibit-worthy. Perhaps the library where you meet would like a show!

- Use the meeting commitment as an incentive to create new work to show at every meeting. Remember: quantity generates quality. Keep working!

Some Final Words

Jean asked our eight students to comment on a variety of issues. Their words provide inspiration and food for thought, and may resonate with your own experiences.

On Creating . . .

I am a planner when I create my quilts. However, I still follow Lorraine's suggestion to "make visual decisions visually." These decisions along the way can change the final outcome. – Abbi

Creating is so confidence building. It permeates other areas of my life. – Amalia

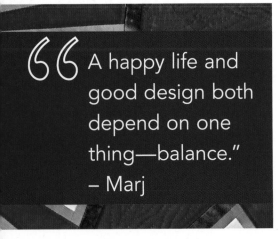

"A happy life and good design both depend on one thing—balance." – Marj

I feel all humans have to make something with their own hands. If they don't, they are not fulfilled and they die early. – Jane

Creative voice is a style of expressing yourself through art. I have several voices and I have not yet settled on my one creative voice. – Ruth

On Your Inner Critic . . .

People deny themselves many opportunities to create because they believe they can't do it. – Jane

I am my own worst critic. It is hard for me to start unless I have things all figured out. – Bonny

My inner critic resides in the logical, judgmental side of my brain. The longer I stay in my studio and become absorbed in the piece I am creating, the easier it is to quiet that voice. – Amalia

I don't do my best if I worry about what others want or expect. – Jane

I'm not good at silencing the critic. It may just happen in shifting from left brain to right brain. – Ruth

On Inspiration . . .

I sketch all the time. Life without drawing and graph paper would be like life without food to me. – Jane

I set goals. If I waited around for inspiration, I would probably eat or read a magazine. I force myself to start even when I don't feel inspired. – Abbi

Be open! – Jane

I think there are many opportunities available to us to be inspired. I used to think there weren't any, but now I think I just wasn't paying attention. – Marj

When you limit yourself in your resources you find more creative ways to use the materials. – Ruth

On Designing . . .

Technique doesn't affect my design decisions. I just find a technique that works. – Abbi

When I learned how important value was in a quilt, I realized that one reason my quilts weren't satisfying was inappropriate use of contrast in value. – Amalia

" When I began quilting and didn't know much, I was more productive. Now, with knowledge, I am more creative." – Cindy

I don't plan any of my work. It is a completely intuitive process. – Cindy

As I sketch, I am looking for a shape I love. When I find it, I add other elements to that shape until I find something I like. – Jane

I don't think I had a strong intuitive sense of values, colors, texture, and scale. The process of learning the basics has given me a lot of confidence. – Marj

I am more of a planner when I design. But my ideas always change as I go along. When the critic in me says, "That's not working," I find another way. – Ruth

I have developed the sketching habit. I used to jump quickly from sketch to cloth, but in the University of Washington Experimental College's Fiber Arts Certificate Program I participated in, I was given the assignment to come up with an idea and sketch it 50 times. And I was surprised; my favorite sketches were not in the first 25. – Sharon

On Vision . . .

When I finish a quilt and give it away, I don't care what happens to it. The pleasure for me was in the making of it. – Amalia

My work is my way of getting my message out into the world. I am not evangelical, but I have my hopes for the world. My art is the way to get my message out there. – Sharon

When I make something for someone, I am thinking of them as I make it. I hope they will look at it and think of me. Otherwise, I feel it is irrelevant what happens to my work when I am gone from this earth. – Ruth

On Time . . .

I made time (to work/sew) even though I was working two jobs. – Abbi

It is important to allow yourself time to create. Giving myself that time allowed me to connect to a community and be around others who value and support art and creating. – Ruth

> " I don't let much take me away from my artwork. I make time."
> – Marj

On Process . . .

When I am away from my quilting for a few weeks, I have a hard time getting started again. It is difficult to break through the inertia barrier. – Bonny

Some people say they can't. I say try. – Jane

I always start with a design idea. When I finish it may not look like the idea I started with, but having an idea helps me start. – Marj

Technical aspects of creating are always on my mind. But I learned from my dad that there's always a way to make it work. Design first, then think of the technique. – Ruth

A big blank wall is overwhelming to me, so I do small fabric sketches. They may not have anything to do with my next project, but they keep my juices flowing. – Sharon

On Working in a Series . . .

I don't know all the possibilities of a series until I am working in it. – Abbi

So far, my series are very short. I don't get very far into a series before I am distracted by a new idea. – Bonny

On Critique . . .

In exposing myself to critiques, I feel I have nothing to lose. Critique can only improve my work. – Bonny

At first the critiques were very hard for me. I worried that others wouldn't like what I did. Now I want the advice, and I take it home and use it. – Amalia

The most useful critiques (of my own work) often pinpoint the flaws that I know are there but would rather not face or can't verbalize. I'd like people to be harder on me and push me further. – Bonny

In critique groups, I feel it is important to be with people who are designing at all levels and who do different work than I do. To grow as an artist I need this exposure. – Sharon

> " Being part of a design group provides stimulation and a safe place to risk and receive honest critique Without these I could not progress in my art." – Jane

About the Authors

LORRAINE TORRENCE was an art major in college and has an MFA in sculpture. Six months before graduating, she made her first quilt and has pursued quilts and wearable art as her primary medium since 1971. She teaches nationally and locally, judges wearable and quilt shows, owns a wearable art and quilt pattern business, and has designed a line of fabric. In addition to her books with C&T Publishing, she has republished *Design Essentials: The Quilter's Guide* (available at www.lorrainetorrence.com). Lorraine lives in Seattle with her husband, near their two grown children and two grandsons. Contact Lorraine at www.lorrainetorrence.com.

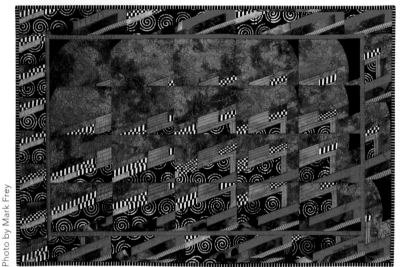

Also from C&T Publishing by Lorraine Torrence

For patterns, books, fabric and more:
www.lorrainetorrence.com

Different Points of View, Lorraine Torrence, 2005, 36″ x 24″

JEAN BRAUTIGAM MILLS is a fiber artist, life coach, and psychotherapist of 28 years. She has a master's degree in clinical psychology with an emphasis in art therapy. Jean uses the creative process is all aspects of her work to help others heal and find new avenues for personal expression. A native of the Northwest, she is currently residing in Omaha Nebraska, where she creates her fiber collage work in a shared fiber art studio and gallery. She has facilitated creativity workshops in Santa Fe and Ireland, and is currently teaching fiber collage and design classes in Omaha and Seattle. Jean can be reached through her website at www.jeanbmills.com.

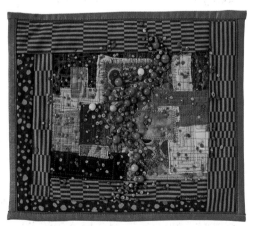

Carnival, Jean B. Mills, 2005, $9^7/_8$″ x $8^3/_8$″.

Great Titles *from* C&T PUBLISHING

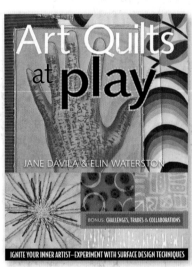

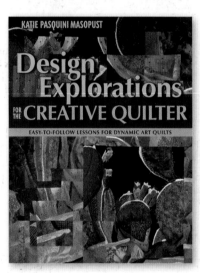

Available at your local retailer or **www.ctpub.com** *or* **800.284.1114**

For a list of other fine books from C&T Publishing, ask for a free catalog:

C&T PUBLISHING, INC.
P.O. Box 1456
Lafayette, CA 94549

(800) 284-1114

Email: ctinfo@ctpub.com

Website: www.ctpub.com

C&T Publishing's professional photography services are now available to the public. Visit us at www.ctmediaservices.com.

For quilting supplies:

COTTON PATCH
1025 Brown Ave.
Lafayette, CA 94549

Store: (925) 284-1177

Mail order: (925) 283-7883

Email: CottonPa@aol.com

Website: www.quiltusa.com

Note: Fabrics used in the quilts shown may not be currently available, as fabric manufacturers keep most fabrics in print for only a short time.